THE ENGLISH NOVEL

THE
ENGLISH NOVEL

From the Earliest Days
to the Death of
Joseph Conrad

by

FORD MADOX FORD

CARCANET

First published in 1930.

This edition published by
Carcanet Press Limited
4th Floor, Conavon Court
12–16 Blackfriars Street
Manchester M3 5BQ

Reissued in new format in 1997.

A CIP record for this book
is available from the British Library.
ISBN 1 85754 358 0

The publisher acknowledges financial assistance
from the Arts Council of England.

Printed and bound in England by SRP Ltd, Exeter.

CONTENTS

This book was written in New York, on board the S.S. *Patria*, and in the port and neighbourhood of Marseilles during July and August, 1927. For the purpose of rendering it more easily understood by the English reader I have made certain alterations in phrases, in Paris during the last four days of 1929 and the first two of 1930.

CHAPTER ONE

THE FUNCTION OF THE NOVEL
IN THE MODERN WORLD

I

O<small>NE</small> finds—or at any rate I have always found—English History relatively easy to grasp because in it it is not difficult to see a pattern of what some one has called Freedom slowly broadening down from precedent to precedent. One may or may not agree with the statement, one may or may not like the fact, if it is a fact, that it sets forth ; but at least it gives us that pattern, some sort of jumping-off place, something by which one may measure and co-relate various phases of the story. The histories of most other races are more difficult to grasp or follow because they are less systematized and more an affair of individuals. One may be aware that the pre-Revolution history of France is an affair of power gradually centralizing itself on the throne, and that

[1]

the Fronde was an episode in that progression. Nevertheless, the Fronde with its violent personalities, its purely individual intrigues, its Cardinals, Queens, Condés, Chevreuses and the rest, was a baffling affair to follow, and obscures the issue which doubtless was that, all power being concentrated under one hat, the neck which supported the head which supported that hat was easy to strike off.

But when it comes to the History of Literature—and to that of the Novel in particular, almost the exact inverse is the case. Whereas almost every country other than England—or indeed every race other than Anglo-Saxondom—has a tradition of literature in which some sort of precedent broadens down into some other, it would appear that however docile the Anglo-Saxon may be in the hands of politicians or leaders—usually of a Leftwards complexion—the moment any æsthetic discipline proposes itself for his direction he becomes at least as refractory as any Condé and almost more intriguing than any Chevreuse.

Any sort of English writer takes any sort of pen and on any sort of paper with in his hair whatever sort of vine-leaves you will and at his elbow any nectar from metheglin to

Chateau Yquem or pale ale, writes any sort of story in any sort of method—or in any sort of mixture of any half-dozen methods. So, if he have any of the temperament of an artist, you have a Fielding or a Trollope, a Samuel Butler or a George Meredith, each rising as a separate peak but each absolutely without interrelation with any other.

That was never better exemplified than quite lately when you had—all living simultaneously but all, alas, now dead—Thomas Hardy, George Meredith, Henry James, Joseph Conrad, and Mark Twain. Each was a considerable figure but each sat, as it were, alone on his little peak surrounded by his lay satellites, and each was entirely uninfluenced by the work of all the others— two solitary Englishmen, two Americans and one alien. Whether or no there was any resultant literary movement I am about to try to trace for you, looking at the matter with the eyes of a craftsman surveying his own particular job.

In the case of any other country or race such a proceeding would be comparatively easy. In France, for instance, living at the same time as, but all predeceasing, the distinguished Anglo-Saxons and the alien of genius that I have named above, you had Flaubert, Maupassant, Turgenev, the Goncourt brothers, Gautier, Daudet—six Frenchmen and an alien of beautiful genius. They all met frequently, dining together almost weekly at Brébant's—where Henry James in the wake of Turgenev dined from time to time too. With amiability, with acidity, with passion or frenzies of hatred they discussed words, cadences, forms, progressions of effect—or the cannon-strokes with which one concludes short short-stories. They were during those meetings indifferent to fame, wealth, the course of public affairs, ruin, death. For them there was only one enduring Kingdom—that of the Arts—and only one Republic that shall be everlasting: the Republic of Letters.

The resultant literary movement—for with their deaths it crossed the Channel—I shall endeavour to trace, and the enterprise will concern itself with the modern English novel. For the Art of Writing is an affair as international as are all the other Arts—as International, as Co-operative and as mutually uniting. Shakespeare could not have written as he did had not Boccaccio, Petrarch, and Plutarch preceded him, nor could Flaubert have written *Madame Bovary* as he wrote it had there not been before then the *Clarissa Harlowe* of Richardson. Nor yet could Conrad have written *Heart of Darkness* or *Lord Jim* had Flaubert not written *Bouvard et Pécuchet* or Alphonse Daudet, *Jack.*

It is, at any rate, in this spirit that, in this small monograph, I shall present to you my reflections on the English Novel—which is the same thing as the Novel—and the pattern that, for me, it seems to make down the short ages during which it has existed. It will differ very widely from the conclusions arrived at—and above all from the estimates formed by—my predecessors in this field who have seldom themselves been imaginative writers let alone novelists, and who, by the exigencies of their professions, have usually been what it is the custom to call academic. That I cannot help. For the benefit of the reader who wishes to know what is generally thought of these subjects I have tried to state along with my own differing conclusions what that general thought is. If, I mean, I belabour the winking lewdness of *Tom Jones*, I am careful to point out that most of my professional predecessors or contemporaries beatify Fielding because of his refreshing carelessness in most matters to which decent men pay attention. The young, earnest student of literature for professional purposes should, if he desires good marks, write in his thesis for examination pretty well the opposite of what I have here set down. But, in the end, it is as useful to have something that will awaken you by its disagreements with yourself as to live for ever in concord with somnolent elders. It gives you another point of view, though you may return to the plane from which you started. I was once watching a painter painting a field of medicinal poppies which from where he sat appeared quite black. Suddenly, he grasped me by the wrist and dragged me up a small hill. From there that field appeared dark-purple shot with gold. I said : " It doesn't make any difference, does it, to your composition ? " He answered : " No, it doesn't make any difference, but I wish the d—d things would not do it, for, when I have finished, I shall have to come up here and do them all over again ! "

2

Since the day when Thackeray obsequiously apologized to the world and his readers for being a mere novelist, in the interests of a pompous social system which decreed that the novel should not be seriously regarded and the novelist himself be stigmatized as something detrimental to good order and the decorous employment of spare time—since, then, Thackeray poked fun at the greatest of all his books which may well be regarded, if you will, as the greatest work in the English language, an immense change has occurred in the relative place accorded to the Novel in the Anglo-Saxon social cosmogony. Because, as novelist, Thackeray felt his social position insecure, he must attempt to retrieve himself by poking fun at his book and so proving that at least he did not take the Novel seriously, his heart being in the right place be his occupation never so ungentlemanly. So he must needs write his epilogue as to the showman rolling up his marionettes in green baize and the rest of it.

To-day, however, even the most fugitive of novelists takes his work more seriously and, perhaps all unconsciously, the public accords to the more serious amongst the novelists an attention that formerly it accorded solely to politicians, preachers, scientists, medical men, and the like. This is because the novel has become indispensable to the understanding of life.

It is, that is to say, the only source to which you can turn in order to ascertain how your fellows spend their entire lives. I use the words " entire lives " advisedly.

In older days—dating back to improvement in locomotion—it was possible for anyone, whatever his station, to observe, at any rate roughly as it were, a complete cross-section of the lives from cradle to coffin of a whole social order. In England up to the days of the stage-coach, families were planted on the land practically to all eternity and even within my memory it was nearly impossible for the agricultural labourer to move from one parish—nay, from one farm to another. One of the most vivid of my souvenirs as a boy was seeing a ploughman weep on a great down. He was weeping because he had five children and a bad master who paid him thirteen and six a week and he was utterly unable to get together the guinea that it would cost him to hire a farm wagon and move his sticks of furniture to another and better farm. Nevertheless that man knew more about human lives and their tides and vicissitudes than

I or any other town-dweller in an age of shiftings.

He could follow the lives of local peer, local squire, doctor, lawyer, gentleman-farmer, tenant farmer, butcher, baker, barber, parson, gamekeeper, water-warden, and so on right down to those of the great bulk of the population, his fellows and equals. He could follow them from the time the kid-glove was affixed to the door-knocker as a symbol of birth and until the passing-bell heralded their disappearance into the clay in the shadow of the church-walls. And although that was more emphatically true in Great Britain, the first home of the English novel, it was almost equally true—*mutatis mutandis*—of the earlier settled colonial districts in the United States. Until, say, the early forties of the nineteenth century it must have been almost equally difficult to remove from Rochester, N.Y., as from the Rochester of Dickens, and as difficult to move from the Birmingham that gave to the world the word Brummagem as a term of contempt, as from the Birmingham in a Southern State of the North American Republic.

Then, with ease of locomotion came the habit of flux—which is infinitely more de-

veloped to-day in the United States than
in Great Britain. In London and the urban
districts that house by far the greater bulk
of the English population the prevalence of
the seven years' lease has hitherto tended to
anchor families in one spot for at least that
length of time, but even that space is not
sufficient to give a family much insight into
the lives and habits of its neighbours. In
any case it is significant that novel-reading
is almost infinitely more a permanent habit
in the United States than in Great Britain,
and the position of the imaginative writer
in so far more satisfactory.

In observing a social phenomenon like the
novel these social changes must be considered. The fact is that gossip is a necessity
for keeping the mind of humanity as it were
aerated and where, owing to lack of sufficiently intimate circumstances in communities gossip cannot exist, its place must be
supplied—and it is supplied by the novel.
You may say that for the great cities of
to-day its place is taken by what in the
United States is called the "tabloid" and
in England the "yellow" or "gutter"
Press. But these skilful sensational renderings of merely individual misfortunes, neces-

sary as they are to human existence and sanity in the great cities, are yet too highly coloured by their producers, and the instances themselves are too far from the normal to be of any great educational value. An occasional phrase in, say, a Peaches-Browning case may now and then ring true, but the sound common sense of great publics is aware that these affairs are too often merely put-up jobs to attach any importance to them as casting light on normal human motives.

The servant of a country parsonage leaning over the yew-hedge giving on the turnpike and saying that the vicar's wife was carrying on something dreadful with Doctor Lambert might convey some sort of view of life, ethics, morals, and the rest to another young woman; but the minute dissection by commonplace-minded reporters of the actions and agonies of a lady who essays first unsuccessfully to poison her husband and finally dispatches him with a club— these minute dissections are not only usually read with a grain of salt, but not unusually, too, they are speedily forgotten. Scenes on the other hand presented with even a minimum of artistry will remain in the mind as long as life lasts : *Ivanhoe* must permanently represent mediaevalism for a great proportion of the inhabitants of the globe, though Scott was a very poor artist; and the death of Emma Bovary will remain horrific in the reader's mind, whilst the murder of yesterday is on the morrow forgotten.

It is this relative difference in the permanence of impression that distinguishes the work of the novelist as artist from all the other arts and pursuits of the world. *Trilby*, for instance, was no great shakes of a book in the great scale of things, but an American gentleman asserted to me the other day that that work did more to cosmopolitanize the populations of the Eastern States than any movement of an international nature that has been seen since the Declaration of Independence. I don't know if that is true, but it usefully puts a point of view—and I am not the one to deny it.

It is, in short, unbearable to exist without some view of life as a whole, for one finds oneself daily in predicaments in which some sort of a pointer is absolutely necessary. Even though no novel known to you may exactly meet your given case, the novel does supply that cloud of human instances without which the soul feels unsafe in its adventures and the normal mind fairly easily discerns what events or characters in its fugitive novels are meretricious in relation to life however entertaining they may be as fiction.

That the republic—the body politic—has need of these human-filtered insights into lives is amply proved by the present vogue of what I will call novelized biography. Lives of every imaginable type of human being from Shelley to Washington are nowadays consumed with singular voracity, and if some of the impeccable immortals are in the upshot docked of their pedestals there can, I think, be little doubt that, in the process, the public consciousness of life is at once deepened and rendered more down to the ground. And the human mind is such a curiously two-sided affair that, along with down-to-the-ground renderings, it is perfectly able to accept at once the liveliest efforts of hero-worshippers, denigrators, or whitewashers. The amiable mendacities of the parson who gave to us the little axe and the cherry-tree are to-day well known to be the sheerest inventions; the signal reputed to have been given at the battle of Trafalgar is far more soul-stirring than the actual rather stilted message that Lord Nelson composed. And even if Henri IV of France never uttered his celebrated words about the chicken in the pot, humanity must have invented them—and that too must have been the case with the cherry-tree. In the days when these catch-phrases received world-wide acceptance the public was in fact doing for itself what to-day is left to the writer of fiction.

For the practised novelist knows that when he is introducing a character to his reader it is expedient that the first speech of that character should be an abstract state-ment—and an abstract statement striking strongly the note of that character. First impressions are the strongest of all, and once you have established in that way the char-acter of one of your figures you will find it very hard to change it. So humanity, feeling the need for great typical figures with whose example to exhort their children or to guide themselves, adopts with avidity, invents or modifies the abstract catchwords by which that figure will stand or fall. What Nelson actually desired to say was: " The country confidently anticipates that in this vicissitude every man of the fleet will perform his functions with accuracy and courage ! "—or something equally stiff, formal and in accord with what was the late eighteenth-century idea of fine writing. Signal flags, however, would not run to it : the signaller did his best, and so we have Nelson. Had the signal gone out as Nelson conceived it, not Southey nor any portraitist could have given him to us. Or had Gilbert Stuart's too faithful rendering of the facial effects of badly-fitting false teeth been what we first knew of Washington our views of the Father of His Country would be immensely modified. But the folk-improved or adopted sayings were the first things that at school or before school we heard of these heroic figures of our self-made novel, and neither denigrator nor whitewasher will ever much change them for us, any more than the probably false verdict of posterity on John Lackland who had Dante to damn him will ever be reversed.

As to whether the sweeping away of the humaner classical letters in the interests of the applied sciences as a means of culture is a good thing or a bad there must be two opinions—but there is no doubt that by getting rid of Plutarch the change will extraordinarily influence humanity. Ethics, morality, rules of life must of necessity be profoundly modified and destandardized. For I suppose that no human being from the end of the Dark Ages to the beginning of the late War—no human being in the Western World who was fitting himself for a career as member of the ruling-classes— was not profoundly influenced by that earliest of all novelist-biographers. And, if you sweep away Marcus Aurelius as altruist-moralist, the Greek Anthology as a standard of poetry, Livy as novelist-historian, Cicero as rhetorician, and Pericles as heaven-born statesman, you will make a cleavage between the world cosmos of to-day and that of all preceding ages such as no modern inventions and researches of the material world have operated. For though swiftening of means of locomotion may have deprived humanity of knowledge of mankind, it did little to change the species of generalizations that mankind itself drew from its more meagre human instances. Till the abolition of classical culture in the Western World the ruling-classes went on measuring Glad-stone or the late Theodore Roosevelt by Plutarchian standards—but neither post-1918 King George V nor any future President of the United States can hope to escape by that easy touchstone. From the beginnings of industrialism till 1918 we went on rolling round within the immense gyrations of buzzings, clicks, rattles, and bangs that is modern life under the auspices of the applied sciences ; we went on contentedly spinning round like worms within madly whirling walnuts. But as a guide the great figure had gone.

There is not only no such figure in the world as Washington, Nelson, or even Napoleon—but there is no chance that such a figure can ever arise again. Nay, even the legendary figures that remain have lost at least half of their appeal. A statue of Washington adorns the front of the National Gallery in Trafalgar Square, but it is doubtful if one in a thousand of the passers-by have even heard of the axe and the cherry-tree, let alone knowing anything of his tenacity, single-mindedness, and moral courage. And who in the North American Republic has heard of Nelson and his signal ? For the matter of that, as I have elsewhere related, a young lady science graduate of a very distinguished Eastern University was lately heard to ask when she caught sight of the dome of the Invalides : " Who *was* this Napollyong they talk so much about here?" Of course pronunciation may have had something to do with that. But it was in 1923 that the question was asked, and since then a popularizing novel-biography of Napoleon has had an immense vogue in the United States.

Nevertheless it is to be doubted if ever again figures will be known to the whole world. It is possible that my distinguished namesake is so known because of his popularization of a cheap form of transport, and there are prize-fighters, aviators, and performers for the cinema. But these scarcely fill in the departments of public morals and ethical codes the places that used to be occupied by Pericles, Cicero, and Lucius Junius Brutus.

I am not writing in the least ironically, nor in the least in the spirit of the *laudator temporis acti*. We have scrapped a whole culture; the Greek Anthology and Tibullus and Catullus have gone the way of the earliest locomotive and the first Tin Lizzie. We have, then, to supply their places—and there is only the novel that for the moment seems in the least likely or equipped so to do. That at least cheers me, my whole life having been devoted to the cause of the Novel—I don't mean to the writing of works of fiction but to the furthering of the views that I am here giving you.

One must live in, one must face with equanimity, the circumstances of one's own age. I regret that the figures of Tibullus and our Saviour do not occupy on the stage of the lives of men the place that they did in the days of my childhood—but I have courageously to face the fact that they do not. For it is obvious that it is not to the parson and hardly to the priest that one would go for counsel as to one's material life; still less could the spirit of Alcestis' address to her bed inspire the young woman to-day contemplating matrimony.

In short, if you look abroad upon the world you will see that the department of life that was formerly attended upon by classical culture has to-day little but the modern work of the imagination to solace it. And that the solace of Literature and the Arts is necessary for—is a craving of— humanity few but the most hardened captains of industry or the most arrogant of professors of Applied Science will be found to deny. Our joint Anglo-Saxon civilization to-day is a fairly savage and materialistic affair, but it is also an affair relatively new and untried. It is perhaps more materialistic than was the civilization of Ancient Rome and a little less savage than the early Dark Ages. But both these former periods of human activity had in the end to develop arts and that, it is probable, will be the case with us. The Romans, it is true, relied for their arts mostly on Greek slaves or on such imitators of the Greeks as Horace and Virgil, and the Dark Ages almost solely on Church-men who led precarious existences in hidden valleys. But the respective futures of these Ages are worth considering for our present purposes. For the break-up of the Roman Empire for which innumerable reasons have been found by innumerable pundits remains at least as mysterious as it was before the first ancestor of Mommsen first dug up his first tile and upon it wrote his first mono-graph. Mommsen, to be sure, used to tell us that Rome disappeared because it had no Hohenzollern family to guide its destinies —and that may be true enough. Gibbon ascribed to Christianity the Fall of the Roman Empire and People; others of the learned have laid that catastrophe at the door of difficulties of communication, of the lack of a modern banking system, of the want of organization of the system of Imperial Finances, or of a mysterious and unexplained slackness that overcame alike the Western and Eastern Empires—a slackness due to the pleasures of the table, the wine-cup, of sex and the like.

But we, as upholders of the Arts, the Moralist having been pretty well blotted out as a national or international factor by the avalanche that in 1914 began to overwhelm alike classical culture and revealed religion, we then might just as well ascribe the Fall of Rome to the inartistic materialism of the true-Roman citizen as to any other cause. For the function of the Arts in the State —apart from the consideration of æsthetics —is so to aerate the mind of the taxpayer as to make him less dull a boy. Or if you like, it is by removing him from his own immediate affairs and immersing him in those of his fellows to give him a better view of the complicated predicaments that surround him. A financier, that is to say, who turns from the bewildering and complicated antics of a maze of tape from tickers, or a realtor who turns from the consideration of corner lots and the tangled and exhausting intrigues

that shall make the new boulevard of his
city run through land controlled by his
interests—both these pillars of the modern
State may be expected to return as it were
with minds refreshed if, taking a short respite
from their arduous and necessary tasks, they
lose themselves for a moment in the consideration of the adventures and predicaments
of the *Babbitt* of Mr. Sinclair Lewis or the
attempts at escape from the chair of the central
character of Mr. Dreiser's *American Tragedy*.

I permit myself to mention the works
of friends of my own because I must have
illustrations for my theme and those illustrations must be works of to-day of sufficient
likelihood to last long enough not to be
forgotten at the next fall of the leaf—and
Mr. Lewis and Mr. Dreiser are so much
more my personal friends than immersed in
my own particular little technical swim that
they are more apposite to my immediate
purpose than would be, say, the authors of
The Sun Also Rises or of *My Heart and My
Flesh*—or of *Ulysses*.

3

Arrived at that particular five-cornered
plot in the territory of the Novel I have

foreshadowed the end of this small monograph. For, having traced the gradual course of the development from Apuleius to Joseph Conrad, having followed it from the Rome of Petronius Arbiter to the Spain of Lope da Vega, to the London of Defoe and Richardson, to the Paris of Diderot, Stendhal, and Flaubert—with side glances at the Cockaigne of Thackeray and Dickens and the Russia of Turgenev, Dostoieffsky and Tchekov—and back again to the London of Conrad, Henry James, and Stephen Crane— which last two writers America will not whole-heartedly accept as American, whilst England won't accept them at all—having followed the devious course of the thin stream of development of the novel from the Mediterranean to the Bay of Biscay, from the Bay of Biscay to the Port of London and so backwards and forwards across the English Channel, I shall leave it and you with a bump and with some regret at the gateway to the Middle-West—say at about Altoona. For it is there that the Novel, throughout the Ages the poor Cinderella of the Arts, is nowadays erecting itself into the sole guide and monitor of the world.

I should like to have allowed myself to

say a few words about the modern Middle-Western development, which is for the moment the final stage, of the art to whose furtherance I have obscurely devoted my half-century of existence. But I am condemned like Moses only to perceive that Promised Land. This is a monograph on the English Novel—which includes *The House of the Seven Gables* or *What Maisie Knew*, not on the Middle-Western Novel of to-day which very emphatically doesn't include—oh, say *Riceyman Steps* and *Mr. Britling Sees it Through.*

I should like to observe for the benefit of the Lay Reader, to whom I am addressing myself—for the Professional Critic will pay no attention to anything that I say, contenting himself with cutting me to pieces with whips of scorpions for having allowed my head to pop up at all—to the Lay Reader I should like to point out that what I am about to write is highly controversial and that he must take none of it too much *au pied de la lettre.* I don't mean to say that it will not be written with almost ferocious seriousness. But what follows are suggestions not dictates, for in perusing this sort of book the reader must be prepared to do a great deal of the work himself—within his own mind.

If I choose to write that great imaginative literature began in England with Archbishop Warham in the sixteenth century and ended with the death of Thomas Vaughan, the Silurist, in the first year of the eighteenth century, to come to life again with Joseph Conrad and the Yellow Book about 1892, and once more to disappear on the fourth of August, 1914—if I choose to write those extreme statements it is because I *want* the Reader mentally to object to them the names of Swift, Keats, Thackeray, Browning, Swinburne, Meredith—or even those of Messrs. Galsworthy, Bennett, Wells and, say, Virginia Woolf. I *want* the Lay Reader to make those mental reservations for himself. I should hate to be a professor, I should hate to be taken as dogmatizing, and I should still more hate that what dogmatizing I do perforce indulge in should be unquestioningly accepted by any poor victim.

So that if I should say—as I probably shall —that, along with all his contemporaries, as a constructive artist even of the picaresque school, Dickens was contemptible, or if I say that Meredith as a stylist in comparison with

Henry James was simply detestable, or that the conception of novel-writing as an art began for Anglo-Saxondom with Joseph Conrad, or that *Babbitt* dealt a shrewder blow at the pre-war idealization of the industrial system and the idolatry of materialism than *Don Quixote* at sixteenth-century vestiges of the chivalric spirit, or that *The Time of Man* is the most beautiful individual piece of writing that has as yet come out of America, or that *The Lighthouse* is the only piece of British—as opposed to English—writing that has latterly excited my craftsman's mind—the only piece since the decline and death of Conrad . . . if I commit myself to all these statements the reader must at once violently object that I am a log-roller writing up my personal friends—though I never knew, or even know anyone that knew, Miss Virginia Woolf. He must object that I have forgotten not only Trollope in my aspersions on mid-Victorian novelists, but that I have also forgotten Mr. George Moore. (Alas, I always forget Mr. George Moore, who is probably the greatest and most dispassionate technician that English Literature has ever seen.)

He must make all these objections for himself as violently as possible: then, in reaction, thinking it over he will probably find that there is something in what I say. At any rate, he will have a sort of rudimentary map of the Kingdom of the Art of Letters in his mind. The old-fashioned maps had their advantages. Their cartographer left in his plans blank spaces in places where his enemies dwelt and labelled them : " Here be Crocodiles," " Here be Stenches ! " or " Anthropophagi !   Avoid this Land ! "—and that was useful because it told you what parts of the earth were pernicious to that type of Cartographer.   So, if you were of his type, you avoided territories by him miscalled. On the other hand, if you disliked the sort of fellow that that map-maker was, you adventured into the territory labelled " of the Anthropophagi " to find it inhabited solely by sirens, into the Land of Stenches to find it distinguished by the most beneficent of chalybeate springs, or amongst the Crocodiles, who were charming people, ready at any moment to shed tears over your depleted pockets, your lost loves, or your rheumatic-gout!

It is with a map of that sort that I am trying to provide you.   No other sort is of the remotest value.   Nor is it even possible, critics being human.

I am looking at the last page of a Manual of English Literature compiled by a critic who takes himself and is taken very seriously indeed. I read :

"*His work often decadent, appealing to senses ; a pessimist. Lacks restraint ; small variety in mood !*"

Think of that as the last word—the very last word—of a Manual of English Literature for the use of the English Classes of the most numerically attended University in the Universe ! Could I at my worst do worse ? Or so badly !

For that is that writer's critical estimate —that is all that thirty thousand pupils of a State University are given as an appraisal of—Algernon Charles Swinburne !

CHAPTER TWO

TOWARDS DEFOE

IT is not part of my purpose—nor within the scope of a short manual would it be possible!—to trace the influence of the *Golden Ass* or the *Satiricon* on the course or development of the novel—and indeed their influences probably came into action so late that the effect was rather to give coloration to the pastiches of later writers like the late Mr. Walter Pater or the very much living Mr. Ezra Pound. It is the same, to all intents and purposes, with such mediaeval compilations of short-stories as the *Decameron*, the *Heptameron* or the *Cent Nouvelles Nouvelles*. The *Decameron* must in particular have been as enormously read in the course of centuries as *Madame Bovary*, but, except for the *Heptameron* and the rest of the works of that tradition, it can have led to no developments but merely to a few imitations such as the *Contes Drolatiques* of Balzac.

To our immediate purpose they are germane solely as indicating the desire—the necessity—that humanity has always experienced for fiction of one kind or another, if merely as an expedient for clarifying the mind. The mediaeval European intellect seems to have been able to appreciate these crystallizing shocks only in smallish doses, and in Europe it was not until sixteenth-century Spain that humanity seems to have been able to sustain its interest for the course of a long tale—a series of rambling incidents in the life of one or of one or two central characters. And again it was not until the middle nineteenth century in France and the very late nineteenth or early twentieth that in England the mind of the public could be expected to take in the rendering—not the narrating—of a work whose central character was not an individual of slightly superhuman proportions. Still less could it take in an Affair whose participants, as befits a democratic age, if not all exactly equal in the parts they play in the Affair's development, are at least nearly all as normally similar in aspirations, virtues and vices as is usual in one's surrounding humanity.

Let us for a moment consider the difference

—if difference there be—between the apparently artless tale and the novel that fulfils my definition of the functions of the work of fiction in the modern body politic. The artless tale, then, is nothing but a *conte*—a thing told to keep the hearers gasping or at least engrossed. Told verbally it is usually short, but professional story-tellers have been found—as in the case of the group-authors of the *Arabian Nights*—to make them very long indeed. And the habit of telling very long tales that are practically serials still persists in Eastern bazaars.

You may say that listening to tales for the mere purpose of being thrilled or engrossed has nothing to do with the gaining of vicarious experience, so that the stories of the *Decameron* or the ordinary novels of commerce were and are of no value to the body politic, but a little reflection will show that the reverse is the case in practice. Human experience is built up by the averaging out of a great many cases—some inclining, as it were, to the extreme right, some to the extreme left, and the majority probably approaching the normal.

Personally, on the face of it, I ought to be glad if, in the interests of non-commercial literature, the novel of commerce could be suppressed, but as a matter of fact I should be the first to lament such a catastrophe. Humanity, in fact, needs care-free entertainment—and in search of it it seldom goes very far wrong. That is proved by the fact that, ever since books were books, the great public has devoured with avidity only two kinds of work—the very worst from the point of view of the literary artists, and the very best! The four most popular books the world over at any given moment since, say, eighteen-sixty have always been the *Pilgrim's Progress*, *Madame Bovary* and two sempiternally changing works of egregious silliness and popularity. But whereas the so-called popular books change with the turn of each year, the more serious works continue to stand at the head of the best-sellers of the world year in and year out.

That is a consideration to which we may return; the point that I wish to make here is that when *contes* and *nouvelles* of the type to be found in the *Decameron* were of an almost boundless popularity, not only had the serious novel no existence but the reprehension that the Victorian moralist and industrialist expressed also found then no expression. As I am never tired of relating, my grand-aunt Eliza was the first utterer of the famous saying: "Sooner than be idle

I'd take a book and read "; but that utter-
ance, perfectly normal and applauded about
1860 when it was first presented to the world,
is to-day purely risible and could not in serious
earnestness be uttered in the household of any
family more comfortable in its circumstances
than those of the lower-paid manual labourer.

It would have been equally unthinkable
at any date from the tenth century to the
early nineteenth. During those nine centuries, in fact, the professional moralist was
only too glad to enlist the services of the
fiction-teller under the sacred banners of
Faith and Good Works, and although towards
the end of the eighteenth century the habits
of young ladies who lay day-long on sofas
reading the thousandfold novels of popular
female authors from Aphra Behn to Sarah
Fielding—although that habit was lightly
satirized by dramatists and occasionally
scourged in the sermons of nonconformist
divines, these occurrences were very sporadic
and altogether too infrequent to form a
national habit. Indeed, until the nineteenth
century was under way it might even be
advanced that the writers of such works
of fiction as the *Pilgrim's Progress*, *Rasselas*, or
Robinson Crusoe were eagerly sought as allies

by the professional, ecclesiastical, or nonconformist moralist.

And that was even more pronouncedly the case in days still earlier when in Europe a universal and all-powerful church dictated the morals of gentle and simple alike. Indeed, whatever may or may not be said of Catholicism in the way of praise or blame, it cannot be alleged that when she was all-powerful she was ever afraid of the Arts or afraid to employ them for her own purposes. The Moralities of the Nun Hrotswitha, the mystery plays and mummings of every town-guild in the Middle Ages, are alone overwhelming evidence that the church, representing the professional moralists of five or six centuries, was only too glad to avail itself of forms of art as an indispensable means of spreading her teachings. Nor indeed until the Puritan Divines of the sixteenth and seventeenth centuries turned upon the art of fiction as presented on the stage did that form of art do anything other than bend itself willingly to the services of morality. For you might say that the drama of Wycherley and Killigrew was as much a protest against the oppression of the then professional moralist as any spontaneous movement for the supply of lecherous fiction to the public. The greater part of the plays of the Elizabethan and Jacobean dramatists— by far the greater part—consisted of works of profound—and quite conventional—moral purpose; the earlier drama, and even the pace-egging and mumming of country shows, were nothing but pietistic pronouncements put as picturesquely—and as alluringly spiced with alliterations in the prosody and low comedy in the plots—as the fiction-writers of the day could contrive. Hell always yawned before the audience beneath the high trestle-boards and stages of these shows; in the flies Heaven and its denizens were always visible, whilst in what would to-day be called the wings there waited perpetually visible, on the one hand the Devil ready to pitchfork the wicked into the lower story of the stage —and Man's Good Angel to conduct him to the Better Place. And clowns and characters called Vices were always ready to endure the drubbings that, enlivening the public, were the portion of the mildly wicked and foolish.

No, decidedly the mediaeval and early renaissance art of fiction, quite as much as Matthew Arnold, was on the side of the angels.

It might be as well here to point out that

until the Restoration and its comedies brought scenery and attempts at scenic realism to the stage, the Play and the Novel were practically the same form. Or it might be better to put it that the Novel was the direct development of the play—a development made possible by the art of printing. In effect the plays of Shakespeare were novels written for recitation, and that, naturally, was still more the case with the works of Shakespeare's predecessors. And it is significant that as reading became more common with the establishment of Edward VI's grammar schools, the play itself became less a matter of rantings and by degrees even a medium for fine writing. *Gorboduc* and *Ferrex and Porrex* or *Ralph Roister Doister* were products of either a stilted classicism or of a boisterous, native spirit of knockabout buffoonery, puns, and ribald jests. The classical motive issued presently into a mode of over-written elegance that speedily proved itself unreadable : then Lyly gave place to Shakespeare.

It has always seemed obvious to me—as a private conviction for which I have no wish to do battle and which I have no wish to force on the reader as any more than a suggestion—that Shakespeare himself regretted the literary chastity of his muse. I mean that Shakespeare, as gentleman and one wishing to sport his coat-of-arms in the very best social and scholastic circles, deprecated the passing of the Unities and of bombast and wished that the popular taste would have let him make a living by verse in the style of the *Rape of Lucrece* and the more florid poems that decorate the last pages of editions of his works. His speeches to the players in *Hamlet* and all his life as far as it is known would seem to indicate that. But it is not until you can bring yourself to regard not merely the plays of Shakespeare but the whole post-Lylian Elizabethan and Jacobean drama as novels written for recitation that the great mystery of Shakespeare's life seems to become reasonably explicable. For the great mystery of Shakespeare as novelist is simply : " Why did Shakespeare never correct his proofs ? "

Beside this amazing enormity all questions as to the identity of Mr. W. H. or the Dark Lady or Mary Fitton or of the motives of the sonnets become paler and more ineffectual than any ghosts. For they at least don't matter. But that the greatest writer of all time should not have taken the trouble ever to read his own works in print, preferring to retire to Stratford, sue out his coat armour and so, on his profits as theatre owner, become titularly and legally a Gentleman—that, if you think about it and have ever known an author, is the most amazing phenomenon known to the history of Literature. Napoleon at St. Helena, renaming himself Monsieur Dupont and shuddering at the mention of Austerlitz, would not be more astonishing. For this novelist never blotted a line and never saw his work through the press !

On the face of it the plays of Shakespeare read extravagantly well but, on the modern stage, play extravagantly badly. I have never in my life been more bored and appalled than at having to sit through an uncut performance of *Hamlet*, given by the most noted performers in the world in front of a gigantic real castle. It was terrifying and it lasted from nine at night till four in the morning. There was the real castle, the real moon, real armour dating back to Shakespeare's days, real banners of the epoch ; real soldiers played the troops of Fortinbras—and to add a touch of reality of another sort, in the middle of the performance real Communist groundlings demonstrated for Saccho and Vanzetti !

But the point was that, with the real castle,

pump and the rest, all Shakespeare's descriptions became intolerable pleonasms and gave a singular unreality to the characters that uttered them. For normal humanity does not talk of patines of bright gold when considering the night skies : it says " Look at the stars," and possibly adds : " Aren't they jolly ? " The stars in fact do the rest : and in this given case the castle of Avignon, the Rhone, and the moon were admirably prepared to replace all that anyone's descriptions could do.

On the other hand, I have never in my life been so overwhelmed as by a ranted performance given by capable actors in modern dress in a rather bare modern studio that had galleries round it—a condition pretty well reproducing that of the Shakespearean stage. Hero and heroine and subordinate characters bellowed rhetorical periods, floods of bombast ; they threw their arms about, raved, fell down, and staggered to their feet. The effect, as I have said, was overwhelming ; no such other utter tragedy has ever presented itself to the world for three hundred years ; the grief of the heroine was so insufferable that you could not sit in your place ; when the hero died you groaned aloud. Yet the play was only Kyd's *Spanish*

Tragedy, ranking as a pretty poor work and to-day very difficult to read.

Shakespeare, on the other hand, does read extravagantly well through the greater part of his work—but large portions of the plays must pay the penalty of all works intended for one medium and presented in another. The sheer silliness of many—of most of his plots except in the Chronicle Plays—their sheer silliness and negligence regarded from the point of view of the art of the novel, become technical merit when it is a matter of recitation ; bareness of plot is then a necessity, the mind having no time to turn back and pick up merely suggested clues. And of course a great deal of his work must have seemed to a man of his own delicacy of temperament much more the merest writing down to the groundlings or coarse flatterings of those in authority than that caviare to the general that he hoped to provide.

So that his inattention to the printing of his plays may very conceivably have proceeded from sheer disgust at them—a frame of mind not unfamiliar to the artist when viewing his work in the light of his own ideals. Or of course it remains open to us —all things in the case of Shakespeare being

open to us—to consider that he really regarded his work as commercial trivia that
had much better be ignored in the later stages
of his aggrandizement to the state of gen-
tility. That frame of mind is so usual in
the British novelist and ever since novels have
been translated or written in England has
proved so disastrous to the art itself that it
is quite conceivable that the first—and the
greatest—of them all may have shared in
that national characteristic.

Be that as it may, the assertion that the
Elizabethan and Jacobean play answered in
advance the call from the public for the novel
that was so soon to come may very well be
regarded as fact. And indeed the same may
be regarded as true of all pre-Elizabethan or
rather pre-Edwardian English literature. Or
it might be more just to say that, the Grammar School spreading at once the capacity and
the taste for reading, the enhanced national
wealth of the age of Drake and countenanced
piracy in Elizabeth's day made the purchase
and dissemination of books a possibility
amongst a very much wider class of the public.

We may then regard the rule of thumb
definition of the novel as a printed book
of some length telling one tale or relating

the adventures of one single personage as reasonably acceptable. In that case you get an instance at once of supply created by demand and of that supply being rendered possible by the fact that education and material production arrived almost hand in hand. For although printing was available as a means of spreading knowledge almost a couple of centuries earlier, the exiguity of material wealth and leisure, the turmoil and the scarcity of labour of the centuries of pestilence, dynastic wars, and turmoil that preceded the firm establishment of the Tudors on the throne infinitely delayed and indeed indefinitely put back the clock of culture in these kingdoms.

Roughly speaking, we may say that Chaucer, the first English writer of sustained imaginative pieces, was also the first English writer for the Press—a writer, that is to say, for the individual reader in his closet rather than a composer of lays, ballads, roundels, or even epics, for recitation. The dictum should be accepted with caution. That it is on the whole just is nevertheless demonstrable by the comparison of the *Canterbury Tales* or *Troilus and Cresseide* with say the *Faerie Queene* or Drayton's *Polyolbion*. That the work of Chaucer is readable, whereas the epics of Spenser and Drayton practically defy perusal, is not merely a matter of difference of greatness in the respective authors. Chaucer was an infinitely greater writer than either of his successors : his character-drawing is extraordinary, his sense of beauty overwhelming, his minutely observing mind stalls off the possibility of dullness in his pages. And read to himself by an individual reader the work of Spenser is intolerably pompous, allegorical and dull, and that of Drayton all too pedestrian because of his lack of any powers of selection. But, if you will read the longer works of Chaucer aloud you will find him a little difficult to follow simply because of that very minuteness of observation and that very lack of dullness; the others, on the other hand, gain immensely by reading aloud or by recitation—both Spenser and Drayton taking on a sort of jolly robustness that is even to-day by no means disagreeable and that may well have been enormously engrossing in the mouth of a good reader reading to audiences that had little to do but listen and lacked the power of reading for themselves.

In the matter of the consumption of literature, in fact, the English world had gone back several generations between the ages of Chaucer and Spenser—if, that is to say, you regard the evolution of the printed book and the arrival of the novel as Progress, for it is quite open to you to regard the disappearance of oral poetry and the epic as retrogression. Nevertheless, it is fairly true to say that Chaucer with Caxton, the first printer, as an intimate wrote far more definitely for the Press than did any of the Elizabethan imaginative writers. Except in the internal style and the outward effect of his work there is of course no evidence that Chaucer considered definitely that the coming of the printing press called for a change in the technique of the imaginative writer—but it would not be utterly fanciful to imagine that he did at least consider himself a writer destined to have a great number of individual readers rather than vast audiences destined to listen to recitals of his work.

To what extent I am right in advancing the suggestion that Eastern and Eastern-European audiences had tougher brain-stuffs than their Anglo-Saxon contemporaries, at any rate in the matter of listening to recitals of tales in prose or verse, the reader may decide for himself. The suggestion is nevertheless handy as presenting a certain not unuseful image. We may say that the printing press killed alike the epic and all forms of metrical romance, or we may say that the epic and the metrical romance are essentially foreign to the taste of the Occidental reader —and the second statement is in effect merely a repetition in other terms of the first.

Into that I do not propose to go. It is sufficient to say that when I do make the assertion I find myself, as it were unexpectedly, in company with the academic critic of to-day and yesterday. At any rate, quite orthodox authorities have not unusually asserted that Romaunts or Romances were, in England at least, intended for the personal reading of the mediaeval courtly and clerical individual, whilst the shorter lays, virelais, ballads, and the like were aimed, as being less fatiguing, at popular and numerous audiences. This seems to be merely common sense. On the other hand, very long metrical or prose compositions did simultaneously appeal to Oriental audiences and it is not unusual in academic circles to describe the *Canterbury Tales* themselves as " Oriental in origin," which seems queer but may for the moment pass.

What, however, I am anxious to establish —at the risk of a certain prolixity—is the fact that an appetite for fiction amounting also to an expression of a necessity has, at least since the Dark Ages till the present day, distinguished all humanity. The reason probably is, as I have already hinted, that we need accounts of human life not so much as matter from which to draw morals for our own particular cases but rather as something that will take us outside ourselves and, as it were, to a height from which we may the better observe ourselves and our neighbours. The moral is usually thrown in by the moralist who nevertheless insists or at any rate asserts that moralizing is the sole purpose of his life and work. But the Morality Plays of the Nun Hrotswitha, the Mysteries of every English town from Salisbury to Lytham, the terrifically moralizing novels from *Guzman d'Alfarache* to the history of *Moll Flanders*, were simply evidence of the fact that humanity did not want moralizing and did want fiction. They represent the moralist throwing up the sponge and trying to get a pinch of salt on to the tail of that difficult bird, man. It is obvious that large audiences in days of complete boredom could be found for the sermons of ranting monks and violent reformers. But even at that the appeal was largely fictional and what the audiences went to hear—as was the case with, say, Savonarola—was rather semi-hysterical and lively descriptions of the sufferings of souls in eternal flame than any doctrinal discourses on the life and teachings of Him Whose message was: "Neither do I condemn thee!"

So, gradually, fiction emerging with timidity from under the wing of the Church itself took such prentice flights in the direction of pure rendering of life as picaresque novels like *Don Quixote*. It is, however, doubtful if the adventures of the knight of la Mancha would have got past the Index had not the Church been called in in the person of the parish priest who in the end burns the poor hero's books of romance; and from that point of view Cervantes may be regarded as simply drawing the cord of conventional morality closer round the necks of the unfortunate public. The romance of *The Seven Champions of Christendom* had to be burned not because it was a silly book but because its morality was insufficiently puritan, the Church of Rome in the throes of the Catholic Reaction having to prove itself at least as puritan as the Anabaptists of Münster. So the body that tolerated Rabelais good-naturedly had to invent an *auto da fé* in order to deal with Amadis de Gaul ; and Cervantes, for all the world like a seventeenth-century Thackeray, had to attune his satire to the pipe of a reacting church. Fiction, in short, had to pay an always greater tribute to morality as it escaped from being the mere servant of established religion.

In effect the Church—and then the Churches —said to the novel, the play, the romance, and the ballad : " We are too busy cutting each other's throats and inventing newer theologies, to bother any more about artistic productions. In the meantime we will remove the benefit of clergy that used to shield those who could manipulate a pen. You may write and compose what lay fictions you like, but the rack, the faggot or the pillory will attend you if you publish anything that we *don't* like." And the novelist, always a timid creature and in England avid of social consideration, was quick to take the hint. So Don Quichotte de la Mancha, the only gentleman produced by the genius of Cervantes, and indeed by all the genius of that age, had to become a pitiable lunatic. Yet it is impossible that a man of the perspicacity of the writer of that work could not have seen that the Don, wiping curds from his

[48]

benign and tranquil countenance, was god-
like in comparison to the crooks and gross
peasants—the cats and monkeys!—that surrounded him. Nevertheless the Don must go!

With those Spaniards, then, the novel approached some sort of rendering of life and
that sort of rendering was soon enough to
make its appearance in England. It crossed
the Bay of Biscay and the Channel with a
picaresque work of a prodigious popularity
in its day—*Guzman d'Alfarache* or the *Story
of a Rogue*. Less picaresque in the true sense
of being the strung-together life of a *picaro*
or professional thief—less picaresque than
the immortal *Lazarillo de Tormes* and less
achingly tragic as a presentation of the life
of the brothel and wine-shop than *Celestina*,
the work of Hermann Alemannos, whose
name betrays his Teutonic origin, was much
more suited to the Anglo-Saxon taste than
either one of the other three Spanish books
that I have selected for mention.

The true Spanish genius is for us obviously
too austere. Our public could, it is true,
guffaw over the discomfitures of the knight
of the Woeful Countenance and the manœuvre
by which Lazarillo gets rid of his blind master
who himself was the most ferocious of

scoundrels ; and the suicide from the tower in *Celestina* may have excited disagreeable emotions in the English reader who preferred to think that punishment for sins was a matter of the hereafter. But the remorseless, essentially Spanish black and white of the greater novels was no more for the English public or the English litterateur than are *Titus Andronicus* and *Pericles* when they can get the *Comedy of Errors* or the *Midsummer Night's Dream*.

Guzman d'Alfarache, on the other hand, was a wilderness of enormous passages of trite morality enlivened here and there with episodes of cozening and purse-cutting and it has always been a matter of speculation to me —for I have known these works ever since I was a very small child—to what extent the seventeenth-century public really liked the moralizings, to what extent it was merely hypocrisy, and to what extent, again, readers were really tricked by the tiny ha'-pennyworth of sack into consuming the intolerable quantity of very dry bread. Obviously in the seventeenth and eighteenth centuries mere length was not a deterrent, because there was an immense amount of time for vacant minds to fill in and relatively very few books. So that just as in distant colonies we will read home newspapers with all the advertisements they contain three and four times over, so the subjects of the James's, Charles's, and early George's would accept almost anything that could be read or listened to and probably from being attuned to prolixities they would have disliked anything crisp if anything crisp had been to be found.

That is perhaps a vain speculation, but a short consideration of the first great English novelist, who was for a time at least nearly solely novelist, would lead one to believe that such was indeed the case. Defoe was born about the time of the restoration of Charles II —that is to say, in 1660 or 1661—and died in 1731, aged in consequence about seventy. And it is interesting to note that his novels were all produced in the last twelve years of his life— as an expedient for procuring bread and butter after bankruptcy produced by too ingenious speculations both financial and philosophical.

That gets rid of the theory we might otherwise have entertained that he was a Restoration novelist in the sense that the friends of Charles II were Restoration dramatists. Nevertheless, the active portions of Defoe's life were so passed in the seventeenth century that it comes naturally to think of him rather as Jacobean than Georgian or eighteenth century. It is, that is to say, not in the pomposity of the eighteenth century that Captain Singleton or Colonel Jack or Moll Flanders seem to be clothed. They were rather mobile, swaggering, piratical creatures seated on barrels and smoking their yards of clay than strutters in brocades and ruffles. And probably Defoe's ideal was the substantial London merchant, sturdily planted over his stout calves on square feet. That was his ideal because he had himself lamentably failed in attaining to it.

His financial ideas are said to have found favour in succeeding ages ; his plans for increasing the national revenues, like Swift's, it is said, would have been admirable could they have been adopted. So his moralities are practical rather than theological—it was to the respectable suffrages of the merchants that his pious passages addressed themselves. Thus his moralizings may have been less hypocritical than those of most of his contemporaries, his predecessors or descendants ; but the aspiring after respectability was none the less as marked.

What, however, is in him the most interesting from our special point of view of tracing the development of the art of the novel is the fact that Defoe may be called the first English or foreign writer to strive after some sort of satisfactory convention for the novel. He aimed, that is to say, at being convincing—at convincing his reader that he was reading of real adventures set in the, as it were, official biographies of real individuals. Such fictitious documents as *The Apparition of Mrs. Veal*, the *Memoirs of a Cavalier*, or the *History of the Plague in London* are very near to historic forgeries and ought perhaps to be regarded as fictitious journalism. For, whatever else he was or wasn't, Defoe was the first great journalist.

His *Review of the Affairs of France*, which was a periodical news-pamphlet devoting itself to foreign affairs and what to-day we should call Town Topics, was no doubt Defoe's introduction to fiction. When, that is to say, foreign news ran out he filled in his space with the chronicles of an invented Scandalous Club and there, a little in the style of La Bruyère and still more in the style of the later *Tatlers*, *Ramblers*, and *Spectators*, he presented the Town with slightly scandalous anecdotes of characters purely fictitious or suggested faintly by well-known living men.

From that to inventing false news as in the

case of the *Mrs. Veal* fascicule and from that
again to the production of sham autobiography
like *Robinson Crusoe* is a very obvious progression. Few journalists would make it
to-day, but to-day news being more common
is more easily checked. Be that as it may,
there is no doubt that, whether it were his
intention or no, he did evolve a convention
for fiction that up to a certain point was effec-
tive enough. That he intended so to do
there is not, as was on the other hand the
case with his great successor Samuel Richardson, any evidence. On the contrary, there
is a good deal of evidence that several of his
works of fiction were really intended as
mystifications or frauds on the public.

That does not interfere with the artistic
merit of his work, which was very great.
For whether you set out to hypnotize the
public into believing for the time being that
they have attended at a scene, or trick them
into believing that they have read real memoirs
when the memoirs are fictitious, the artistic,
if not the ethical, results are nearly equal.
There is, however, this difference :

If you should read *Salammbo* and should
be asked if you had ever been in Carthage
before its destruction by the Romans you

might almost answer in the affirmative with truth, whereas in the same scale of things if you were asked if you had been present at the Fire of London and had read Defoe's *History* you could not answer more than that you had read a very authentic account by an eye-witness. And inasmuch as an authentic rendering—a rendering made with extreme artistic skill—will give you more the sense of having been present at an event than if you had actually been corporeally present, whereas the reading of the most skilful of literary forgeries will only leave you with the sense that you have read a book, the artistic rendering is the more valuable to you and therefore the greater achievement. I once heard a couple of French marine engineers agreeing that although they had traversed the Indian Ocean many times and had several times passed through, or through the fringes of, typhoons, neither of them had ever been in one till they had read Conrad's *Typhoon*. And indeed I have myself had the singular experience of looking out at dawn from a tent-flap and seeing the tents of a sleeping army running up into deep woods. And having just been reading Stephen Crane's *Red Badge of Courage*, which opens with the description of the dawn breaking on the tents of a sleeping army, for some minutes I was confused, not being able to understand why the one or two men that I saw about were dressed in our khaki instead of in the blue of the Federal troops of the United States during the Civil War. That is what I mean by saying that one might answer with truth that one had been present at a rendered scene although one might never physically have been present there. For to me it is certain that I was at that given moment more present at the preparation of a battle somewhere near Gettysburg in the 'sixties of last century than actually amongst British troops in support at a battle that was then proceeding in the Belgian Salient in September, 1916.

To produce that or similar effects is the ambition of the novel of to-day.

Two centuries before—by, say, 1716—the novel had proceeded but a very little way. I should say that Bunyan in the *Pilgrim's Progress* and still more in *The Holy War* had gone as far as any writer till that day and dying in 1688 he anticipated Defoe as novelist by at least a generation. Ostensibly the *Pilgrim's Progress* is an allegorical work just as the English Bible is a theological or even

[56]

a doctrinal one ; but just as in the Morality Plays which were produced by professionally religious writers or actors and the Mysteries which were religious spectacles produced and acted under the direction of clerics by members of the professedly lay Guilds—just as in those productions the real attraction was the imaginative presentation of realities rather than the pious aspirations of authors or producers, so it is strongly to be suspected that the realistically human appeal of the *Pilgrim's Progress* far outweighs the moral or religious interests. Indeed in *The Holy War*, which is an allegorical presentation of the eternal struggle between the unseen forces that make for good and evil on earth, the presentation of seventeenth-century warfare is for long passages so realistic that one might accuse Bunyan of having thrown up the moral sponge and of taking a pagan pleasure in fighting for fighting's sake. He renders, in short, battles of the Great Rebellion in which he took part or on whose outskirts he was present. He rendered them and did not write about them.

But the moral fervour and fierce sincerity of Bunyan are so far above suspicion that the mere fact that at times he was carried away in a sheer outburst of the artist's spirit and love of terrestrial aspects for the mere sake of those aspects—his moral fervour is so great and so deserving of respect that no slightest tang of hypocrisy can attach to him any more than it can attach to the translators of the English Bible. And, if we except Smollett and possibly Samuel Richardson who was the real great precursor of the modern novel, we cannot say as much for any other English novelist who wrote before the later years of the nineteenth century. For it is impossible to absolve such writers as Defoe, Fielding, or Thackeray from the charge of deliberately writing with their tongues in their cheeks passages of virtuous aspirations that were in no way any aspirations of theirs and that in consequence very seriously detracted from the value of their works as art.

With Bunyan that was not the case. He desired to inculcate certain moral teachings and he had the sense to see that the best way to inculcate a doctrine and to get it deep into the brain and marrow of the reader was to make him be vicariously present at scenes the contemplation of which would cause certain moral or practical ideas to arise in the mind. And the deservedly prodigious —the deservedly unrivalled popular appeal

[58]

of the *Pilgrim's Progress* is sufficient testimony
at once to the immense skill and the unpar-
alleledly simple moral fervour of its author.
For the reader attending on the episode of the
Slough of Despond is actually in a bog a little
way away from his native town and the man
who reads of Giant Despair is in all truth con-
fronted with either Gog or Magog of the Lord
Mayor's procession in the very flesh. At any
rate, it is to be remembered that, the world
over, together with the *Imitation of Christ* and
Madame Bovary, the *Pilgrim's Progress* is the most
read book in Christendom. And this we must
put down to the artistic skill—to the power
of presentation and of rendering of the author.

For there is no other criterion of art but
success, and the more lasting the success
the better the art. I wish to strike that note
very strongly because as soon as one begins
to talk about an art misinterpretations come
creeping in and one is at once suspected of
at the least asserting one's possession of
superior knowledges or—let us say—of high-
hatting one's neighbour. Nothing is less true.
The knowledge of the art of novel writing is
open to every one who takes the trouble to
like one book better than another and the literary tastes of men are fairly identical the world

over and throughout time. The great art of
the world is found in books that are familiar
to millions, if not the world over, then, at any
rate, down several ages of several continents.

The difference between Bunyan and his
predecessors is one more than anything of
whole-heartedness and if there is only one
work of fiction—for one can hardly call the
Bible a work of fiction—if there is one work
of prose fiction in England that, written before
the birth of Bunyan, has survived to our time
it is Malory's *Morte d'Arthur* and that survives
because Malory whole-heartedly and unassum-
ingly collected such legends of the Arthurian
cycle as he liked and wrote them down
simply and without flourishes. Otherwise,
none of the pre-Elizabethan prose romances
could to-day be read with any other than
archæological pleasure, nor could any of the
prose fiction which began to be mildly
abundant in late Elizabethan and early Jacobean days. I suppose you might read
Deloney's *Jack of Newbury* with some pleasure
if you were interested in Elizabethan guild
or household mysteries. But I cannot imagine
anyone reading for pleasure either *Euphues* or
Greene's *Menaphon*, either Lodge's *Rosalynde*
or even Sidney's *Arcadia*. One may glance

at them from time to time, more or less in order to keep one's end up against the literary archæologist, but they would all, including *Amadis de Gaul*, prove intolerable as books for " reading in "—to use an old phrase which meant a long, long, engrossed perusal. Nash's *Jack of Wilton* has been compared to *Don Quixote*, but there is no sense in reading the Englishman's satire of forgotten manners when one can re-read Cervantes' satire on things that are at the root of the human heart.

The difference between Malory and the earlier romances or *Euphues* or *Menaphon* is simply the difference in the relative sincerities of their authors. Malory records what a simple mediaeval knight liked and to some extent how he looked at the world : it is modest and, its author being wrapped up in his subject, the work has no eye to the modes of the time—or to displaying the cleverness of the writer. You can engross yourself in the *Morte d'Arthur* if your tastes lie in the least in Malory's direction and, except that finally you may arrive at the conclusion that he was a modest and pleasant gentleman, you need never give the author a thought.

With *Amadis de Gaul* or *Euphues*, on the other hand, you are for ever thinking of the cleverness of the author. And you are meant to think of the cleverness of the author, and so you are in the case of *Rosalynde* and an enormous proportion of the Elizabethan drama. The prose and even the blank verse of that age sparkled with trope, metaphor, image, simile, plays upon words, conceits and every type of verbal felicity, so that the last thing that comes to the mind in the case of almost any work of that age is the subject treated of.

Hundreds of thousands—nay millions—of readers have read the *Pilgrim's Progress* and *Robinson Crusoe* without giving a thought to or even knowing the name of Defoe or Bunyan. I asked the other day in France a child who was reading about Crusoe who had written it and she replied: " Je crois que c'est par . . . par Madame de Ségur . . . Ou non: peut-être, Madame d'Aulnoy. Enfin, je n'y ai jamais pensé." And that is about the highest compliment that could be paid to Defoe. I may as well add the same child's comment on the story itself. She did not much like *Robinson Crusoe* because, she said, the sufferings depicted in it were true. She liked, like all children, to read of sufferings, bloodsheddings, and horrors but only as long as she could believe that they were invented, whereas she was of opinion that the prolonged loneliness and fears of Crusoe had actually occurred. Similarly she found the story of the Crucifixion insupportable. The root of all adult criticism is to be found in those revelations.

As long, that is to say, as a work remains in fashion you can be contented to read it in order to remain in the fashion yourself. It matters very little to you that whereas *Robinson Crusoe* is just *Robinson Crusoe*, or *Othello* just *Othello*, *Euphues* is Lyly's *Euphues*, the *Groat's Worth of Wit* Greene's *Groat's Worth* or the *Spanish Tragedy* Kyd's *Spanish Tragedy*. For it is impossible to talk of almost any sixteenth-century work without prefixing the author's name, if the name is known— simply because the attraction, and even the attraction that it once had, lies and lay in the verbal juggleries of the author. I must have read *Euphues* once at least right through and have looked into it several times—but I have not the least idea what it is all about. And even although I have read Lyly's *Campaspe* once or twice, I remember only that the plot is a classical plot—and the lyric:

> Cupid and my Campaspe played
> At cards for kisses, Cupid paid. . . .

The fact is that with Elizabeth English became a supple and easily employable language and, making the discovery that words could be played with as if they were oranges or gilt balls to be tossed half a dozen together in the air, mankind rushed upon it as colts will dash into suddenly opened rich and easy pastures. So it was, for the rich and cultured, much more a matter of who could kick heels the higher and most flourish tail and mane than any ambition of carrying burdens or drawing loads.

In the end, however, what humanity needs is that burdens should be carried, and provided that things get from place to place the name of carter or horse is of very secondary importance. If it is in the fashion we will go down to the meadow and watch the colts cavorting : but all the while we are aware that the business of words as of colts or of the arts is to carry things and we tire reasonably soon of watching horse-play ! For if I say : " I am hungry," the business of those words is to carry that information to you, and if you read the *Iliad* it is that the art of that epic may make Hecuba significant to you. Consider the prose of Cranmer !

[64]

CHAPTER THREE

TOWARDS FLAUBERT

IT may at first sight seem curious that a section of a small work devoted to the English—and of course the American—Novel should be captioned with the name of a French novelist. But in the first place the art and still more the frame of mind of the Sage of Croisset are so deep-embedded in the art and frame of mind of the English and still more of the American novelist and all thought of the great, Nordic work of " that poor dear Gustave," as Mr. Henry James used to call him, is so cast out of all French literary practices or aspirations to-day that if Flaubert is not an English novelist his Titanic and Norman ghost has no place at all. To state one of those half-truths that are infinitely illuminating, you may say that without *Madame Bovary*, *Babbitt* could never have existed and without *Bouvard et Pecuchet* there could have been no *Way of All Flesh*. For

[65]

all I know Mr. Sinclair Lewis may never have
read a word of Flaubert and I will bet my hat
that, for the purposes of this discussion, the
shade of Samuel Butler would declare that he
knew no French at all. But the point is that,
without those two works in French, those two
national monuments in English could hardly at
this time exist or weigh with the public since
the public would not be prepared for them.

Let us go a step further and declare that
without Cranmer we should have had another
three centuries to wait for Flaubert, Henry
James, Stephen Crane, Joseph Conrad, Mr.
John Galsworthy, and my friend " Red "
Lewis. For without the English Prayer Book
and its follower in date and style the English
Bible, with or without Cranmer's suppressed
preface, and without the followers in date and
style of Defoe, Bunyan, and Samuel Richardson, how should we have to-day any English
prose, novel-form or any English frame of
mind ? Or any Anglo-American Concord
literature ; or any British Empire or any
Anglo-Saxon anything ?

You may say that that is stretching things
a little. And yet I do not know that it is.
Let us make concessions. If you will concede to me my little point about the descent

of the English Novel from Cranmer's prayer book and the English Bible—which cannot matter to you at all, I will willingly concede to you that it was the phraseology if not the doctrine of the Book of Common Prayer and the frame of mind of the Old Testament As By Law Appointed that gave to England the Empire of India and to the world the United States of North America, those two shining products of English stiff-necknedness and non-theological Bible-reading. For how without the Books of Kings could either Clive or, say, Andrew Jackson have found heart or courage to continue in their courses? Of course a thought or so might be given to North's *Plutarch* that was published in 1579.

Be that as it may, what I am here getting at is the fact that preceding and underlying the ornate florescences of Lyly and the prodigious formlessnesses of Spenser and preceding and underlying the incredible verbal felicity and neat plottings of Shakespeare himself went the stream of dogged, menacing prose and the realist's native imagery of those two religious compilations. And that subterranean stream immensely fecundated—to make no larger claim—at once the Anglo-

Saxon national character and the literature that is to be found in the English language.

I am aware that here we are on ticklish ground and that reformers and the advanced generally deny with a great deal of heat that literature has any influence at all on peoples. I remember once being furiously lectured by the most moral and one of the most advanced of English novelists—being furiously and minatorily taken to task because mildly and to make conversation I alleged that *Don Quixote* had something to do with the passing of the sham chivalric spirit in Europe. The lecture was indeed so furious that, being a non-combative person and caring nothing about the matter, I have from that day to this rather given up considering the subject at all. You see, my friend the novelist was so notoriously virtuous and benevolent that hitherto I should have hated to hurt his feelings by advancing that anyone could be influenced by any book at all. For what he alleged, like an apostle announcing some kind of creed, was that populaces influence literature—that Cervantes was produced because a widespread spirit of mockery for chivalry, real or sham, was so abroad in the world that *Don Quixote* was written merely in answer to a demand, as articles on the Calcutta Sweepstake are written about the time when Derby Day approaches.

As to that I am no authority and the reader must settle for himself whether that hen or that egg came first—I mean whether the spirit of the English populace demanded first the English Prayer Book and the English Bible and demanded afterwards in due course the *Pilgrim's Progress* and *Robinson Crusoe*, or whether the English Bible so influenced the English people that they demanded in due course the works of Bunyan and Defoe. Or as a third proposition: Did the English Bible so influence Bunyan and both so influence Defoe that in the end the product was *Pamela*, the short tales of Diderot, the novels of Stendhal, Flaubert, and his successors and so on until the novel of to-day was arrived at?

As I have said, I do not immensely care about the matter. Bunyan may never have read the Bible, Defoe may never have read Bunyan, or Richardson Defoe. But it makes such a convenient pattern to assume that writers are descended the one from the other that I mean to assume it and the reader must modify the theory how he will.

Regarded from that point of view, in pre-

as in post-Elizabethan days and underlying
Elizabethan days themselves, you did have
that stern but decorated prose and that
determination to rely on illustrations, parables,
and images drawn solely from material to
be found about normal people the world
over and throughout time; simultaneously,
on the surface of things you had a courtlier
and more elaborated prose which had the
Sublime as its ideal and nothing less vulgar
than passages modelled on Juvenal or the
plays of Plautus for its light relief. The
Bible says : " Take us the little foxes, the
foxes that eat our grapes " as an illustration
of love, and " He shall feed his sheep " as
the highest expression of the divine function-
ings of the Saviour. The *Faerie Queene* cannot
deal with any fox or any hound of lower
extraction than Cerberus and the only re-
deemer who could have saved the world
for the writers of Romances was, in his
panoply, King Arthur with Lancelot, Gawain,
and the rest of his apostles all pricking over
the plains of Camelot.

So let us say that it was to the homespun
illustrations, the simple imagery and the stern
diction of the Bible that we owe Bunyan—
for obviously Bunyan read the Scriptures,

year in and year out, during a lifetime of
Bedford Gaol, of persecution and turmoil,
whereas the only remains of the courtlier
modes are found to come from North's
Plutarch which influenced profoundly Shakespeare and possibly Sir Thomas Browne.
But Shakespeare obviously could not have
any successors and Browne found none till
R. L. S. came to be his sedulous ape. So
that the influence of North's translation
remained, if profound, at least rather ethical
than literary—until it was finally ousted by
the versions of the Langhornes and Church's
of days much more modern.

Our space not being boundless we must
now skip to Richardson. For Richardson I
have the profoundest respect that amounts as
nearly as possible to an affection—if that is
to say it is possible to have an affection for a
man whose death preceded one's birth by one
hundred and twelve years. I do not apologize
for the fact that *Pamela* is my personal favourite,
whereas the graver critics and mankind in
general prefer *Clarissa*. By that the reader
need not be guided, but he should certainly
pay a good deal of attention to the works of
Richardson—and indeed to Richardson himself.

That tranquil person came into the world

in 1689—twenty-seven or eight years after the birth of Defoe and one year after the death of Bunyan. But whereas both of his predecessors seem to strike notes almost entirely of the seventeenth century, Richardson seems to be absolutely of the eighteenth and, with him, sentimentality was born in the world of the novel. That perhaps was necessary to an age that banished if not conventional, then at least doctrinal, moralizings to its collections of sermons in volume form. For them of course there was a prodigious demand.

Of course, too, it would be wrong to assert that moralizing found no place in the novels of Richardson since the high moral purpose breathes from every pore of his pages. But it was not with moralizing that he made his primary appeal as had been the case with Bunyan, nor was it likely that had he so done he would have found many readers. No, it is his sentimentalizing that is his E string.

Against that I have nothing to say. Anglo-Saxons are sentimentalists before everything and in all their arts, and it is probable that without sentimentality as an ingredient no Anglo-Saxon artist could work : certainly he could have no appeal. To produce national masterpieces in paint Turner must bathe his canvases deep in that gentle fluid; the English lyric is a marvel of sentimentality and so is English domestic architecture with its mellow—or mellowed!—red brick, its dove-cotes, its south walls for netted fruits. So the first of modern novelists must be one of the greatest of sentimentalists. And on those lines his appeal is universal and everlasting.

Only to-day an American left the ship on which I am writing in the port of Lisbon and, I happening to mention because he was in my mind the name of Richardson, this American—professor at that and practitioner of a sister art—this American gentleman assured me solemnly that he read *Clarissa Harlowe* at least twice every year and cried often during each reading. Now there must be some reason for this phenomenon, which appears very singular. It is not, however, rare, for the hottest literary discussions I have ever had in England—where, of course, the discussion of literature is not in good form —have been with laymen like professors or lawyers as to the relative merits of *Pamela* and *Clarissa*.

For me, I read Richardson for a hearty

and wholesome dose of sentimentality and if one does that one may as well have that quality laid on as thickly as it will go. And it seems to me that the history of a serving-maid who resists her master's efforts at seduction and ultimately forces him to marry her is a more sentimental affair than that of a young lady of quality who permits herself to be seduced by a relatively commonplace Lothario. For myself I have always felt inclined to cheer over the success of the one young female rather than to weep for the tribulations of the other. Pamela certainly seems to be the more sporting character of the two.

Still, one should perhaps not read Richardson for his sporting quality, and that sort of thing is really no affair of mine. The main point is that Samuel Richardson is still read and read with enthusiasm. I have even met persons who were engrossed by the conversations in the Cedar Parlour of *Sir Charles Grandison*.

That Richardson's tender muse was at times too much for the robuster and more cynical taste of his age is proved by the fact that Fielding's first famous novel was begun as a parody on the first famous novel of

[74]

Richardson. By that date the novel of commerce was well on the way to the market and young ladies lying on sofas reading the latest fiction or furiously sending their maids to the circulating libraries for the next five volumes of their latest favourite—such young ladies were familiar features of the social landscape. Literature had, in fact, become a sound, if not an immensely lucrative, proposition.

And it is pleasant to think that, happy as he was in everything that he touched, Richardson was not only novelist but printer and publisher and quite a warm business man in either capacity. He was, too, a favourite correspondent and companion of innumerable young ladies who consulted him as to their amatory predicaments and because of that he is not only the first novelist in the modern sense of the word but also the first literary feminist. You might call him an eighteenth-century Henry James and not go so far wrong.

At any rate, he stands alone as a modern novelist and had in England neither appreciable imitators nor rivals until the arrival on the scene of the author of the *Barchester Towers* series.

Except for Smollett—whom it is hopeless to expect Anglo-Saxon readers to appreciate or to consume, the main stream of development of the novel passed once more to the Continent of Europe. Smollett begat Captain Marryat, who was one of the greatest of English novelists and is therefore regarded as a writer for boys, Smollett himself being most prized by the purveyors of books called " curious " in second-hand catalogues.

Before, however, considering Diderot, Stendhal, Chateaubriand, and Flaubert, all avowed followers of the author of *Clarissa*, it might be as well to think a little about Fielding—as at once a dreadful example of how not to do things and as the begetter of Thackeray and the product that it is convenient to call the nuvvle as opposed to the novel. For at about the date of the births of Napoleon, Wellington, Ney, and many others who began the modern world, and just a little after the death of Richardson, and just a little before the birth of the North American Republic, and still a little more before the Cæsarian operation that produced the French Republic, distinct cleavages began to make themselves observed in the fields of writing, these eventually hardening them-

[76]

selves into the three main streams of the Literature of Escape from the everyday world; into the commercial product that Mamma selected for your reading, that it is convenient to call the nuvvle and that formed the immense bulk of the reading matter, and finally into the modern novel which does not avoid the problems of the day and is written with some literary skill. This last Richardson begat.

And it is convenient to say that Defoe, in spite of his moralizations, was the first writer of the Literature of Escape, just as Smollett and Marryat may be described as carrying it on and the young H. G. Wells and the young Rudyard Kipling as bringing it—at any rate temporarily—to a triumphant close.

Were it not that they were avowed moralizers of a middle-to-lower-middle-class type, the Fielding-to-Thackeray lineage of writers might also be regarded as purveyors of the Literature of Escape, but their continually brought-in passages of moralizations are such a nuisance that they cannot be ignored. Though they were both amateurs in the sense that neither knew how to write or cared anything about it, Thackeray at times projected his scenes so wonderfully that now and then he trembles dreadfully excitingly on the point of passing from the stage of purveyor of the nuvvle to that of the real novelist. And it is to be said for Fielding that although *Tom Jones* contains an immense amount of rather nauseous special-pleading, the author does pack most of it away into solid wads of hypocrisy at the headings of Parts or Chapters. These can in consequence be skipped and the picaresque story with its mildly salacious details can without difficulty be followed. One might indeed almost say that Fielding was a natural story-teller, whereas Thackeray was none at all. Fielding at least, like a story-teller in a school dormitory, does manage to lose himself in details of people running into and out of each others' bed-rooms in hotel corridors at night—something like that. But Thackeray never could : the dread spectre of the Athenæum Club was for ever in his background.

And I imagine that the greatest literary crime ever committed was Thackeray's sudden, apologetic incursion of himself into his matchless account of the manœuvres of Becky Sharp on Waterloo day in Brussels. The greatest crime that anyone perhaps ever committed! For the motive of most crimes is so obscure, so pathological or so fatalized by hereditary weakness, that there is almost nothing that cannot be pardoned once one has dived beneath the calm surface of things. But Thackeray as child-murderer can never be forgiven: the deeper you delve into the hidden springs of his offence the more unforgivable does he appear.

I had better perhaps explain the cause of all this emotion for the benefit of the lay reader who has not yet got at what I am writing about.

The struggle—the aspiration—of the novelist down the ages has been to evolve a water-tight convention for the framework of the novel. He aspires—and for centuries has aspired—so to construct his stories and so to manage their surfaces that the carried-away and rapt reader shall really think himself to be in Brussels on the first of Waterloo days or in Grand Central Station waiting for the Knickerbocker Express to come in from Boston though actually he may be sitting in a cane lounge on a beach of Bermuda in December. This is not easy.

Of the three major novelists that we have hitherto examined each in his own way had a try, consciously or unconsciously, at performing this conjuring trick. Bunyan tried to do it—and succeeded remarkably well—by the simplest of story-teller's devices. He just told on in simple language, using such simple images that the reader, astonished and charmed to find the circumstances of his own life typified in words and glorified by print, is seized by the homely narrative and carried clean out of himself into the world of that singular and glorious tinker.

Defoe, on the other hand, in the conscious or unconscious effort to achieve a convention for the novel, adopted the biographical or autobiographical form, relying on the verisimilitude of the details that he invented to confirm the reader in the belief that his characters had really existed and so to awaken the sympathy that makes books readable. And had he possessed a little more power of projection or a little more subtlety in presenting his figures and had his writing been a little less pedestrian his works might have gained and held the power to arouse a great deal more enthusiasm than they actually do.

Richardson, going a good deal further, has left it on record that he was actually bothered by the problem of the novelistic convention

and that he racked his brain a long time before
arriving at the one he finally adopted. He
asked himself, that is to say, how the reader
was to be convinced that the author—and
by analogy still more his characters—how
could they know all the details that go to
making up a book? If, to reduce the matter
to its most elementary form, Sir Charles
Grandison is walking in the Yew Walk, how
can he know what characters are present
and what conversations are being carried on
in the Cedar Parlour, and since, to satisfy the
reader, the author is to be supposed to be
cognizant of all that passes in his novel, how
is *he* to know simultaneously what is happening in both places?

That at least is what bothered Richardson
and what has bothered all other novelists since
his day, though until quite lately no English
novelist made any serious attempt to attack
the problem. The method that Richardson
with characteristically homespun common
sense eventually worked out was simply to
cast the whole novel into correspondence,
the characters exchanging letters as to events
and as to their psychologies with other characters or with anyone to whom a letter could
be handily addressed. In that way any

character who was needed to know anything could be given the information and the author had only to let it be supposed that he had an unusual knack of getting hold of the correspondence of other people to convince the reader for all eighteenth-century purposes. For in the seventeenth and eighteenth centuries, as every one knows, every one from Madame de Sevigné upwards and downwards addressed to every one else letters of prodigious length and in the most excruciating detail—and Richardson himself, as we have seen, had a prodigious knowledge of the prodigious letters that eighteenth-century young ladies could address to even unknown correspondents once their hearts and feelings were touched. So that although to-day the letter is one of the worst of methods that exist for telling a story if the dictates of probability are to be considered, Richardson may be considered to have done very well indeed with his peculiar form.

To its disadvantages in other hands we shall come in due time, but meanwhile enormous applause is due to the author of *Pamela* for having given the matter any thought at all. And in any case his is a figure so sympathetic and so craftsmanlike that we do well to love him. He is sound, quiet, without fuss, going about his work as a carpenter goes about making a chair and in the end turning out an article of supreme symmetry and consistence. I know of no other figure in English literature—if it be not that of Trollope—who so suggests the two supreme artists of the world—Holbein and Bach.

It would be hyperbole to suggest that Richardson is as great in his art as either of the other two. He had neither their power over their materials nor their sense of the beauty of natural things. Our gratitude to him nevertheless should be great, for he worked with the simplest materials and manœuvred only the most normal of characters in the most commonplace of events and yet contrived to engross the minds of a large section of mankind. How to do that is the problem that, Richardson having been dead a century and a half, still engrosses the novelist.

And what more than anything is impressive about his figure is that one knows almost nothing about it: he is as little overdrawn as are his characters, whereas the besetting sin of almost all other English novelists from Fielding to George Meredith is that they seem to cut their characters out with hatchets and to colour them with the brushes of house-painters and, never, even at that, being able to let them alone, they are perpetually pushing their own faces and winking at you over the shoulders of Young Blifil, Uncle Toby, the Widow Wadman, Dick Swiveller, the Marchioness, Becky Sharp, Evan Harrington, and the rest. That is usually applauded by orthodox Anglo-Saxon criticism and to talk of the gallery of portraits left by this or that novelist is considered to be high praise indeed. But, as a matter of fact, the overdrawing of characters is merely a symptom of the laziness and contempt for their vehicle that is the too usual hall-mark of the English writer of nuvvles. And that it should be tremendously applauded is a symptom of the disdain that the English critic really feels for the novel. If English painting consisted of nothing but the caricatures of Rowlandson, Gillray, or Cruikshank, the art-critic would discover very soon that that grew monotonous, but since it is merely a matter of prose-fiction it is easily accepted as good enough ; that which is too stupid to be said in any other way being consigned to the novel.

Of course if you choose to consider Swift

and, say, Beckford as novelists you do arrive at something that you must, as you might say, chew upon—at something that has some mental dignity; and Smollett presents you with problems of humanity that are at least worth consideration. And naturally great vital spirits like Dickens, floundering away in oceans of words and eccentricities, will from time to time hit upon collocations of words and confrontations of characters that are unsurpassed in the literature of any time or nation. But from the death of Swift to the publication of *The Way of All Flesh* there is very little to be found in the English novel that is not slightly unworthy of the whole attention of a grown-up man—say of a grown-up Frenchman.

I have adumbrated somewhere—in some previous pessimism !—the perturbation that must beset any Anglo-Saxon who desired to point out to almost any grown-up foreigner of average intelligence the glories of the English novel before, say, the day of the *Yellow Book*. Let us then examine with a little more attention the chief lights of that Institution between, say, 1745, the year of the death of Swift, and, say, 1890, when the *Yellow Book* was well on the way.

Swift himself is obviously one of those solitary figures like, in their different ways, Shakespeare or Smollett or the author of *The Way of All Flesh*. In a sense he resembles Bunyan, that is to say he wrote allegories which, as a literary *genre*, are usually tiresome and unconvincing; but in his case, as in that of Bunyan, his fierce powers of observation and rendering carry him, as it were, in spite of himself, into the realms of realism. It is to be doubted if Swift ever aimed—as did, say, Mr. H. G. Wells in, say, *The First Men in the Moon*,—at giving the reader the sense of vicarious experience. Nevertheless he got there all the same and the corrosive nature of his misanthropy almost aids the sense of reality with which he overwhelms us. The " purpose " of *Gulliver's Travels* was no doubt philosophic, as the purpose of the *Pilgrim's Progress* was moral; but Lilliput is as real to us as the Slough of Despond and the Yahoos are the figures of the most horrible experience of every man who has come across them.

So that if to your intelligent—and of course slightly cynical—foreigner you presented *Gulliver* and left it at that he might remain edified or horror-struck according as his individual frame of mind were pessimist or the other thing. But supposing you were to present him with the Steele-cum-Addison collaboration of the *Tatler* or the *Spectator* or with *Tom Jones* itself, which was written about a quarter of a century later than *Gulliver* and thirty years or so after the last number of the *Spectator* appeared in 1714 : and supposing you added—yes, certainly, suppose you add *Tristram Shandy* and the *Sentimental Journey*, the first appearing or being written between 1760 and 1767 and the second being published in 1768 ! Keep up your sleeve Tobias Smollett whose *Humphry Clinker* was published three years after the *Sentimental Journey* and in the year of Smollett's death at the age of fifty. And let us conclude this immediate inquiry of ours as ending with the awful name of the Wizard of the North who was born in the year of Smollett's death and lived to be sixty.

As we have seen, Defoe in his *Advice from the Scandalous Club*, that was a " feature " of his periodical *Review of the Affairs of France*, very little anticipated—but by five years, indeed—what may be regarded as the fiction of the Addison-Steele collaboration. One is so apt to regard Defoe as of the seventeenth and Addison as of the eighteenth centuries that this appears rather astonishing, but actually the *Review* ran from 1704 to 1713 and the *Tatler* plus *Spectator* from 1709 to 1714. Defoe's publication was so essentially commercial and the other two so essentially social that the matter is rather one of chronology than comparison.

The fact that the novel had not yet begun as a commercial " proposition " to come into its own reduced Addison and Steele no doubt from the rank of novelists to those of draftsmen of " characters." The novels of Defoe were " faked " memoirs and the other fiction of the period mostly consisted of equally " faked " memoirs of persons of quality, court-mistresses, and the like. And the " characters " and sham correspondence about social questions of the day that characterized the *Spectator* may well be considered as developments of those popular, fictitious productions. Sir Roger de Coverley, Will Wimble, and the rest are as it were the characters of a novel, standing about and waiting for employment as the leaden soldiers of a child await their owner's orders to fall in.

The idea of sustained fiction might indeed, if you liked and if you analysed the matter very closely, be said not by any means yet to have reached the public consciousness, and though for us *Clarissa* may seem to be the first of novels, its peculiar form—of correspondence—may well, in the public mind of its day, have given it the aspect of the last of the spurious memoirs. And, considering the nature of the future influence of Richardson over the French realists from Diderot to Flaubert, it may be more accurate to regard that aspect as the truer one. For, in effect, the French realist movement from Diderot's *Le Neveu de Rameau* to *Le Rouge et le Noir* and again to *Madame Bovary* may in the last event be regarded as much more a movement for the production of fictitious memoirs than the narration of sustained tales, the difference between Richardson, Flaubert, and Joseph Conrad or Turgenev being simply one of form. Richardson, that is to say, tried to assure you that Clarissa was a real person by the mechanical device of publishing her letters, whilst Flaubert and his school try to hypnotize you into believing in their characters by methods of projection rather than of narration.

And the trouble with the English nuvvelist from Fielding to Meredith is that not one of them cares whether you quite believe in their characters or not. If you had told Flaubert or Conrad in the midst of their passionate composings that you were not convinced of the reality of Homais or Tuan Jim, as like as not they would have called you out and shot you, and in similar circumstances Richardson would have showed himself extremely disagreeable. But Fielding, Thackeray, or Meredith would have cared relatively little about that, though any one of them would have knocked you down if they could, supposing you had suggested that he was not a " gentleman." So would any English novelist to-day.

That of course is admirable in its effect on Anglo-Saxon literary-social life where anyone taking pen in hand becomes *ipso facto* an esquire for all users of type-writing machines. But it is bitter bad for the English novel.

It is bitter bad for the English novel because —as is the case with all human enterprises— the art of the novel is so difficult a thing that unless a man's whole energies are given to it he had much better otherwise occupy himself. For if Shakespeare's ambitions for coat-armour had antedated instead of coming after *The Tempest*, where should we be to-day? We have to thank our stars that he was probably first a lousy, adulterous, poaching scoundrel— like Villon !

The lot of the novelist is, in fact, hard— but not harder than that of any other man. If you put it to bakers, tram-conductors, politicians, or musicians that they must be first bakers and the rest and then gentlemen, they will sigh, but admit it. It is almost only the English novelist who will aspire at being first gentleman and then craftsman —or even not craftsman at all since it is not really gentlemanly to think of being anything but a gentleman.

This is an incisive way of putting a truth that might perhaps be more wrapped up in social or material generalizations, but it is none the less a hard truth, and if you consider the case of Fielding, connected with the best families, placeman and diplomatist in a small way, and compare him with Smollett who was socially nothing at all with no chance of a change, you will see that truth all the more clearly.

God forbid that I should say anything really condemnatory of any book by any brother-novelist, alive or dead. One is here to commend all that one can commend and to leave the rest alone. But there are few books that I more cordially dislike than *Tom Jones*. That is no critical pronouncement but merely a statement of a personal prejudice : one may dislike grape-fruit and yet acknowledge its admirable qualities, or one may, as I do, dislike the quality of goose-flesh that reading Mr. George Moore will confer on one's skin and yet acknowledge Mr. Moore as easily the greatest of living technicians.

But as regards *Tom Jones* my personal dislike goes along with a certain cold-blooded, critical condemnation. I dislike Tom Jones, the character, because he is a lewd, stupid, and treacherous phenomenon ; I dislike Fielding, his chronicler, because he is a bad sort of hypocrite. Had Fielding been in the least genuine in his moral aspirations it is Blifil that he would have painted attractively and Jones who would have come to the electric chair, as would have been the case had Jones lived to-day.

Of course that is merely saying that Fielding liked a type that I dislike—but what appals me in view of the serious, cynical foreigner that I have postulated our taking about with us is the extremely thin nature of all the character-drawing, of all the events and of all the catastrophes. Is it to be seriously believed that Tom Jones's benefactor would have turned upon him on the flimsy nature of the evidence adduced against him, or, equally, is it to be believed that Tom Jones's young woman would have again taken up with him after all the eye-openers she had had, she being represented as a girl of spirit? It simply isn't in any world of any seriousness at all. The fact, in short, is that Tom Jones is a papier-mâché figure, the catastrophes the merest invention without any pretence at being convincing and even the mere morality of the most leering and disastrous kind.

For myself, I am no moralist: I consider that if you do what you want you must take what you get for it and that if you deny yourself things you will be better off than if you don't. But fellows like Fielding, and to some extent Thackeray, who pretend that if you are a gay drunkard, lecher, squanderer of your goods and fumbler in placket-holes you will eventually find a benevolent uncle, concealed father or benefactor who will shower on you bags of tens of thousands of guineas, estates and the hands of adorable mistresses—those fellows are dangers to the body politic and horribly bad constructors of plots.

It is all very well to say that such happy

endings were the convention of the day,
that you find them in the *School for Scandal*,
The Vicar of Wakefield and in every eighteenth-
century romance that you pick up out of the
twopenny book-box, and it is all very well
to say that the public demands a happy
ending. But the really great writer is not
bound by the conventions of his day, nor,
if he desires to give his reader a happy ending,
need he select a wastrel like Jones as the
recipient of his too easily bestowed favours.

If, in short, we are to regard Fielding as a
serious writer writing for grown-up people, we
must regard him also as a rather intolerable
scoundrel with perhaps *Jonathan Wild* to his
credit. But *Jonathan Wild* is of another category and, neither winking nor leering, might be
regarded as the finger on the wall, pointing out
what happens to the Tom Joneses of the world
if their case is regarded with any seriousness.

But the fact is that for a century and a
half after the death of Fielding nothing in
the Anglo-Saxon world was further from
anyone, either novelist or layman, than the
idea that the novel could be taken seriously.
It was a thing a little above a fairy-tale for
children, a little above a puppet-play; and,
if not actually as damned socially and cleri-

cally as the actor who could not be either received at court or buried in consecrated ground, the novelist was practically without what the French call an *état civil* because his was not a serious profession. In England that state of things still pertains. In the demobilization forms after the late War the novelist was actually placed in the eighteenth category—along with gipsies, vagrants, and other non-productive persons; and my last public act in Great Britain being to allow my name to be placed on a list of voters, when I gave my avocation to the political agent as being that of a novelist, he exclaimed: " Oh, don't say that, sir. Say ' Gentleman ' ! " He was anxious that his list should appear as serious as possible.

That being the state of things and the novelist being human—for you cannot be a novelist and lack the ordinary aspirations of the human being!—for that century and a half the Anglo-Saxon public had the novels that it deserved. I do not mean to say that generous spirits lacked amongst the ranks of fiction-writers. That great genius, Dickens, thrashed oppressions and shams with the resplendent fury of an Isaiah; and that singular megalomaniac, Charles Reade, did, with *It Is*

Never Too Late to Mend, really succeed in modifying the system of solitary confinement in English gaols. And you have had *Uncle Tom's Cabin*. But those works of propaganda had either no literary value at all or when, as in the case of Dickens, they did have the literary value that genius can infuse into work however faulty, their work itself suffered by the very intensity of their reforming passions.

That tendency alone has deprived the novel in Anglo-Saxondom of almost all the artistic or even the social value that it might have had, since it became a vehicle for preventing the comfortable classes thinking of unpleasant subjects whilst presenting their agreeable somnolences with the warming possibilities of considering their neighbours' defects. It became, that is to say, the week-day, post-prandial sermon preached by a family divine above all anxious to avoid giving offence to those who provided his daily bread. And gentlemanly reformer, the British novelist consciously or unconsciously remains to this day—in the great bulk.

That Dickens, on the other hand, had, any more than Bunyan, any *arrière-pensée* at all should never for a moment be thought. His was an agonized soul shuddering at the tor-

tures that, as a poor child, he had seen inflicted
on the sufferings of non-comfortable humanity
in the horrible days—for the under-dog!—
of the last years of the reigns of the Georges
and of the early years of the reign of Queen
Victoria. All the horrors of insanitation,
filth, child-labour, imprisonment for debt,
the gallows for petty theft, the hulks and the
rest he had himself witnessed or endured and
at these horrors he lashed with the mad
enthusiasm of a wolf that snaps at the insupportable whip of the trainer. His novels
were probably—at least in the beginning—
relatively nothing to him; if he could have
found any other way he would have poured
out his feelings as readily in that. But,
happening on the novel and having a matchless command of English, he took the simple
course of presenting you with villains all
black, heroes all white and ringletted heroines
all pink. He had to see—though that is to
reverse the colours—the world in terms of
Legrees, Uncle Toms, or Amelia Osbornes.

That, in effect, was the beginning of the
end, the novel becoming *the* vehicle for the
reform of abuses. And it is astonishing how
short has been the career of the novel as an
art compared with that of pottery-moulding,

baking, weaving, or any other human avocation. You may say that it began with Richardson and ended—for the time being and as far as Anglo-Saxondom is concerned—with *Oliver Twist*, which, significantly enough, appeared in the first year of Victoria's spacious reign.

Richardson, that is to say, did have an artistic convention of sorts, did try in some way to render life, did deal almost exclusively in neither very moral nor very immoral personages, but there almost all attempts at rendering life or the normal almost came to an end. *The Vicar of Wakefield*, " noted for purity and optimism," says my official guide to dates, was an obviously Richardsonian *pastiche*; Henry Mackenzie's *Man of Feeling* may be said to have exaggerated Richardson's tearful sentimentality; and Smollett (" marked by coarseness and brutality ") whose first book was published eight years after the publication of *Pamela* and in the same year as *Clarissa*, undoubtedly had a shot at rendering the same world that Richardson rendered. It is not as absurd as it may seem to say that *Pamela* suggested *Roderick Random*; it certainly suggested *Madame Bovary*—and *Babbitt*!

It would, however, undoubtedly be absurd to suggest to the public that Smollett was a greater artist or a greater novelist than either Fielding or Dickens : and yet, if the novel is to be regarded as a rendering of life, there is not much way out of it. He remains, however, and will probably always remain, an isolated figure. He was bitter, and as he rendered what he had seen and since what he had seen had been coarse and brutal, those will be the epithets that Anglo-Saxondom will for ever bestow on him. He wrote about the sea in a period glorious for England's sea-history—but in spite of that he could hardly be regarded—as is Marryat—as a writer for boys. The life of which he treated was too remote from to-day for the reader interested in the renderings of the life of to-day to read of it with any enthusiasm ; he was little less virulent than Swift and, if he is even less read, he receives even less lip-service. So no doubt he is contented.

Marryat—as a writer read by boys, men being already too dulled in the sense at twenty to appreciate him—has probably, through the boys, exercised the greatest influence on the English character that any writer ever did exercise. His magnificent gifts of drawing —not exaggerating—character and of getting an atmosphere have so worked that few of us have not been to sea in frigates before the age of eighteen and come in some way in contact with non-comfortable men and women. I have seldom been so impressed as when, the other day, I re-read *Peter Simple* for my pleasure. It was to come into contact with a man who could write and see and feel. For me, nothing in *War and Peace* is as valuable as the boat cutting-out expeditions of Marryat and for me he remains the greatest of English novelists. His name is not even mentioned in the manual of literary dates with which I have just been refreshing my memory.

I do not, however, dwell at any length on either Smollett or Marryat because, great as for me they seem, they still remain individual figures leaving very little trace on the traditions of English literature—and that indeed was the case with Fenimore Cooper who was one of the most beautiful pure stylists that the English language has yet excited into writing. There is in *The Two Admirals* a passage descriptive of mists rising from the sails and cordage of battleships as seen from the turf of cliff-tops at dawn, that remains for me one of the incomparable passages in the language. And, whilst I am about the matter of pure style, I may as well explain here why lately I mentioned that I was then writing in Lisbon harbour. That apparently egotistic excrescence was due to the fact that I liked to remember that—no, not Fielding—but Beckford once lay in Lisbon harbour and wrote most beautiful prose there. Beckford is known only as the author of *Vathek*, which is, to be sure, most remarkable as a *tour de force*—and which is usually bound up with *Rasselas* in popular reprints ; but he is also the author of *Letters from Portugal* which might almost be regarded as a novel, such an admirable autobiographical portrait do they give of their writer in his adventurous progress from the city of Camoens and Vasco da Gama to the monastery of Batalha.

Prose, I suppose, is to some extent the business of a writer on the English Novel, so I suppose I may be pardoned my digression about Beckford and make the note that if I wanted to put together a small, exquisitely pleasing fascicule of admirable because simple English prose I should take a passage from the suppressed Preface to the Bible, a passage from Henry V's address to his soldiers before Agincourt, one from Clarendon, one from *Gulliver*, one from Johnson's *Life of Drake*, the passage from Cooper that I have mentioned above, and

one from the *Letters from Portugal*, one from
Maine's *Ancient Law*—and then one from any
book of W. H. Hudson. The English language
is not very distinguished for its prose, but that
would make a very admirable little volume !
One might almost add the opening description of the village from White's *Selborne*.

It is of course impossible to exhaust the
topic of the English novel from Fielding to
Henry James in a few paragraphs of a small
book. But the topic of main currents of that
literature is more easily got rid of simply
because there are practically no main currents
at all. There are some good writers, but of
a Tradition practically no trace. The writers
who spring most immediately to the imagination as being somewhere near in their works
to the main stream of the international novel
—for the Novel is after all an international
affair—the most unforgettable writers of that
type are two or three women. That I suppose is because, whilst the men ran about
actively intent on proving that they were
gentlemen or in improving the ungentle
world, the women had to prove that they
were not unladylike and so remained at home
and looked at life, without any very immediate
aim at publicity or even at publication.

At any rate, if you take Miss Burney's *Evelina*, Miss Edgeworth's *Castle Rackrent*, Miss Austen's *Sense and Sensibility*, Mrs. Gaskell's *Mary Barton*, George Eliot's *Scenes from Clerical Life*, and Miss Brontë's *Villette*, you do get something of a kinship, if not much of a tradition, and if you add to them the *Barchester Towers* series of Trollope and the works of Mark Rutherford and George Gissing you do get, too, some attempts at rendering English life that are above the attention of adults with the mentality of French boys of sixteen. At rendering, that is to say, rather than at the mere relating of a more or less arbitrary tale so turned as to ensure a complacent view of life and carried on by characters that as a rule are—six feet high and gliding two inches above the ground !

That is, of course, an arbitrary generalization as to all the English nuvvles that string out from, say, Scott to, say, the late Marion Crawford. But if sweeping it is not *completely* unfair. Obviously even Scott's *Antiquary* is worth consideration if one had the time, or *The Cloister and the Hearth*, or let us say *Lorna Doone*. That last work I read over twelve times when I was a boy and from the beginning : " If any man would hear a plain tale told plainly, I John Ridd of the parish of Oare " to the end; I dare say I could recite half the book to-day. But then Blackmore was a market-gardener! Let me lay on his altar these alms for oblivion, for I suppose that few people to-day read of the Doones of Badgeworthy or of how John Ridd took his Lorna home in the great snows.

In short, if you omit Dickens and Thackeray as immense amateurs who wrote from time to time very admirable passages, and if you do not like the works—from *Evelina* to *New Grub Street*—that I have mentioned in my last paragraph but two, the amount of work that you can read in English produced between 1799 and 1899 or so will seem extremely small—supposing you to be of any at all adult tastes or of any seriousness of approach to literary matters.

If, on the other hand, you are indifferent to whether you are convinced by what you read and care little with what you occupy your spare time and desire to fill up your hours with an occupation calling for as little mental concentration as, say, a game of golf, I dare say you could agreeably narcotize yourself still with *Rob Roy* or *The Tower of London* or *The Woman in White* or, say, *Rudder Grange*.

CHAPTER FOUR

TO JOSEPH CONRAD

Thus in Mid-Victorian years there established itself for all the world to see—
The English Nuvvle.

And inasmuch as this phenomenon was really, in the last event, combined—and no doubt unconscious—socio-political propaganda, it was accepted by the whole world —and by the whole world even more than by England. For if, as it were, you shut your eyes and consider what images are brought up before you by the words The English Novel you will see a Manor House, inhabited by the Best People : Sir Thomas, amiable but not bright; Lady Charlotte, benevolent, charitable, in an ample crinoline, an Earl's daughter; the Misses Jean and Charlotte as pure as dew within lily-chalices; Mr. Tom—not absolutely satisfactory; Mr. Edward, always satisfactory; pigeons, short-horns, a rose-garden, a still-room, a housekeeper, a rectory. And you will see a whole countryside, a whole continent, a whole world so conducted that those amiable but not bright personages shall lead amiable, idle, and almost blameless existences in an atmosphere of curtsyings and cap-touchings. It was a world-ideal: you found households modelling themselves upon it in the Government of Kiev, in the State of Massachusetts, in Pomerania, in the department of the Var. So that God's Englishman of the novels of William Black—God's drooping-bearded Englishman with his crinolined or be-bustled consort, carrying fly-fishing rods and croquet mallets, became the type which the whole world sighingly aped. For these nuvvles— to which nobody surely could object—were read in Sarajevo as in Potsdam, in Washington as on the Berkshire downs. They were works written for the would-be gentry by the near-gentry which latter, if their books proved sufficiently acceptable, might almost aspire to such establishments as they described and, in the second generation, to authentic gentry-dom. The writer himself, like Shakespeare, would as a rule have to content himself with a grant of arms from the College of Heralds. But one could always, if one were

a novelist, dazzle one's mind with the idea
that Edward Bulwer Lytton, author of *The
Last Days of Pompeii*, became successively Sir
Edward Bulwer, and Lord, Lytton, and Ben-
jamin Disraeli, also a novelist, Earl of
Beaconsfield and favourite of his Sovereign.

The nuvvles, naturally, differed in subject
and even sometimes in treatment. *The Woman
in White* was, I think, written in letters for
all the world like *Clarissa*; *Esmond*—which
described the founding of a county-family
in Virginia, U.S.A.,—was autobiographical;
or you might have several characters each
speaking in solid autobiographical wads;
or several diarists. There was, in fact, no
literary convention in particular—there was
only the point of view. *Romola* and *Far
From the Madding Crowd* had to be recognized
as of the same ethical family as *Pelham* or
Lorna Doone or they would not do at all.

Occasionally disturbing breaths swept across
the trout-ponds. The newest novel of Thackeray might cause a great deal of trepidating
discussion under the breath, or the latest
passionate outpouring of Dickens might cause
Mamma to ask dear Papa whether Lucy and
Emily ought really to be allowed to read it.
Steerforth and Little Em'ly came *very* near

the Knuckle : but the lap-dog died amongst such lamentations and the first heroine so delicately, and such refined retribution overtook alike Steerforth and the young woman that, if *Copperfield* itself was put on the index of the young ladies' boudoir, *Bleak House* which " introduced Society " could not be kept from the fair denizens of that be-chintzed sanctuary. I believe, however, that *Great Expectations*, the last of Dickens' works to show his passionate compassion for the underdog, had a pretty rough passage.

I came into the world myself at about the hey-day of this national phenomenon, but, by the time I had any real literary consciousness, its supremacy was beginning to be already challenged. My own mother enjoined on me the reading of *Silas Marner*, *The Mill on the Floss*, *Wuthering Heights*, *Sidonia the Sorceress*, *Lorna Doone*, *The Woman in White*, *The Moonstone*, *Diana of the Crossways*, and *Far From the Madding Crowd*. But then my mother was " advanced " and never wore a crinoline. My father thought Dickens was vulgar and though he did not forbid me to read he certainly deprecated my expressing any enthusiasm for—*Bleak House*. He thought too—I don't know why—that Robert Louis

Stevenson was meretricious, except for the *Inland Voyage*. My grandfather, who was considerably more "advanced" than either my father or my mother, first recommended me to read—when I was about seventeen—*Madame Bovary, Tartarin de Tarascon* and *Tartarin sur les Alpes*. He was pleased when at school they gave us the *Lettres de mon Moulin* of Daudet and a little later made me read *Roderick Random, Humphry Clinker, Snarleyyow, Midshipman Easy,* Waterton's *Wanderings in South America,* which was all the same as a novel. My uncle William Rossetti gave me *The Castle of Otranto, Caleb Williams, Frankenstein* and another novel of Meinhold's—*The Amber Witch.* I inherited from my uncle Oliver Madox Brown a large number of translations from the sixteenth- and seventeenth-century Spanish. Trollope I had to find out for myself, oddly enough. I suppose my own family were too advanced to care to advocate the reading of projections of the lives of the cathedral clergy. That, at any rate, was the reading of a boy of from twelve to eighteen of fairly advanced family in the 'eighties of last century. It will be observed that, with the possible exception of Wilkie Collins' two books, these were all works that would not normally be read in Middle Class families, either because of social outspokennesses, individuality of outlook, or difficulties of style. But even for my family it was then possible to go too far. I remember my mother being seriously perturbed because at the age of thirteen or so I was kissed at a tea-party by Mrs. Lynn Lynton whose gleaming spectacles certainly frightened me and whose novels advocated the Revolt of the Daughters of that day—and, if it had lain within the ideas of right and wrong of my family to forbid anyone to read anything, I should certainly have been forbidden to read the works of Rhoda Broughton, who advocated the giving of latchkeys to women.

Nemesis was by then on the way.

The newer ideas began with the cheapening of the products of the press—and I dare say that cheapening was a good deal hastened by the pirating of American works. I remember still with delight the shilling edition—it was bound in scarlet paper—in which I first purchased at the age of fourteen in a place called Malvern Wells, Artemus Ward's *Among the Mormons*, Sam Slick's *The Clockmaker*, Mark Twain's *Mississippi Pilot*, Carleton's *Farm Ballads*, and ever so many other American books which I suppose must have been pirated or they could scarcely have been sold for a shilling. And, though I was ready at the injunctions of my family to read Lope da Vega or Smollett, nothing would have induced me to spend sixpence on taking out from a circulating library the three-volume novels of William Black, Besant and Rice and the other purveyors of the nuvvle when by saving up my pocket-money I could buy for a shilling —or ninepence net—the *Biglow Ballads* or *Hans Breitmann*.

So that of the novel of commerce of those days I really know very little—and I do not think that there is very much about it that anyone need know. That it existed in great numbers in three volumes apiece was obvious. In every little town in England there was in those days a circulating library and in every circulating library in every town were shelves on shelves of obfusc bindings—but even the literary textbooks of to-day give you no more names for the Victorian period than Dickens, Thackeray, George Eliot, the Brontës, Charles Kingsley, Robert Louis Stevenson (who died in 1894), George Meredith and Thomas Hardy. So that even the official list is a pretty meagre one and if I rack my brains really hard I cannot add many names to it. I have already given you Black, Blackmore, Besant and Rice who collaborated—and of writers of considerable merit, Mark Rutherford and Samuel Butler, but neither of these really belong to the period —and Jane Austen really precedes it, though we may well say that she originated the novel of the country-house that was followed— at such great intervals—by the swarm of commercial writers.

That all the commercial writers who solidly turned out solid three-deckers produced absolute rubbish need not be assumed. Miss Braddon, authoress of *Lady Audley's Secret*, did honest, sound journeyman's work, year in, year out, during a very long life—and obviously such a writer as Mrs. Gaskell will not ever be entirely forgotten, if only on account of *Cranford*. I wish, myself, that more weight attached to her *Mary Barton*, a grim—and indeed an extraordinarily painful —account of Mid-Victorian labour troubles.

And of course there is Trollope.

Trollope and Miss Austen—like Shakespeare and Richardson—stand so absolutely alone that nothing very profitable can be said about them by a writer analysing British fiction in search of traces of main-currents of tradition. They were both so aloof, so engrossed, so contemplative—and so masterly —that beyond saying that some people prefer *The Warden* to *Framley Parsonage* and *Sense and Sensibility* to *Pride and Prejudice*, and that others think the reverse, there is very little to be said. These at least are authentic writers : they neither flare out into passages that are all super-genius—as in Dickens' passage about the dry leaves at Mr. Pecksniff's back-door, nor do they descend to the intolerable banalities of the endings of *Copperfield* or *Vanity Fair*. But, as in the case of Turgenev, the aspiring writer can learn very little of either. These novelists write well, know how to construct a novel so as to keep the interest going with every word until the last page—but after that all you can say is that they were just temperaments, and quiet ones at that. Inimitable—that is what they are. You could imitate Oscar Wilde —but never Trollope giving you the still, slow stream of English country and small-town life. Nor could anyone else ever give you such pure agony of interest and engrossment as you can get out of the financial troubles over a few pounds of the poor clergyman in

Framley Parsonage. I shiver every time that I think of that book.

But once those tributes are paid it is astonishing to look back on the course of the novel in England from the earliest times to say, 1895, Bunyan, Defoe, Richardson, Fielding, Smollett, and then the few Victorians of whom we have been treating. It is an astonishingly small crop, even if you let me add Marryat and add for yourselves the other solitary figure of Mark Twain, one of the greatest prose-writers the English language has produced.

In the meantime, across the Channel, the main stream of the Novel pursued its slow course.

It had begun with Richardson. His vogue with the French would be incomprehensible if we were not able to consider that the French Revolution was, in the end, a sentimental movement, basing itself on civic, parental, filial, and rhetorical virtues. If the French beheaded Marie Antoinette it was in order that Monsieur Durand, stay-maker of the Passage Choiseul, might be sufficiently well-fed to utter tearful homilies to his children; for homilies uttered by starving peasants with their bones pushing through their skins and rags—such homilies would little impress their children with the solid advantages of virtuous careers. And the moment you consider pre-revolutionary France from that angle the appeal of the author of *Pamela* becomes instantly blindingly clear.

At any rate, Diderot wrote *Rameau's Nephew* as a direct imitation of that work of Richardson and a whole school of the contemporaries of Diderot imitated *Rameau's Nephew*. The influence, again, of Richardson is plainly visible in Chateaubriand—for without Richardson how could he have written long passages like : " How sad it is to think that eyes that are too old to see have not yet outlived the ability to shed tears," and the like. And if the Richardsonian influence upon Stendhal does not so immediately spring to the eye, we know from Stendhal's letters that it was extremely profound.

It was to Diderot—and still more to Stendhal—that the Novel owes its next great step forward. That consisted in the discovery that words put into the mouth of a character need not be considered as having the personal backing of the author. At that point it became suddenly evident that the Novel as such was capable of being regarded as a means of profoundly serious and many-sided discussion and therefore a medium of profoundly serious investigation into the human case. It came into its own.

It is obvious of course that before the day of Diderot authors had put into the mouths of their characters sentiments with which they themselves could not be imagined to sympathize. But that was done only by characters marked " villain," all the sympathetic characters having to utter sentiments which were either those of the author or those with which the author imagined the solid middle classes would agree. Young Mr. Blifil, Mrs. Slipslop, and the rest might say very wicked things, but they were so obviously wicked and absurd that no one could take them with any seriousness either as pronouncements or as worthy to be taken as the author's opinion : Mr. Allworthy or Amelia Dobbin, on the other hand, could never utter anything without the reader having to exclaim : " *How* virtuous ! " . . . And consider the material success that always awaited the good !

By the time the thirty years or so that stretched between 1790 and 1820 had impinged on the world it had gradually become evident, on the Continent at least, that so many differing codes of morality could synchronize in the same era, in the same nation and even in the same small community—it had become so evident that if Simeon Stylites and Oliver Cromwell were saints, Jesus Christ and Gautama Buddha and several Chinese philosophers were very good men, that the Novel, if it was at all to express its day, must express itself through figures less amateurishly blacked than Uriah Heep and less sedulously whited than the Cherryble brothers.

Changes in literary methods are brought about very slowly and permeate more slowly still into the taste of the more or less unlettered classes who make up the bulk of the desirable readers for an author. As a rule the process begins with the younger writers who find tiresome or ludicrous the accepted work of their day ; a little later the more experienced of readers, tiring in their turn of accepted methods in the works they consume, turn with relief to the younger writers, the professorial and established critics still thundering violently against the younger schools. For, everywhere but in England, schools establish themselves as soon as restlessnesses betray themselves in artistic circles. The more experienced readers, in spite of the critics, spreading abroad amongst the larger classes of the relatively unlettered the taste for the newer modes, at first that larger class become converts and then the professional critics whose bread and butter depends on their following the public taste. So a school is established and for a time holds its own. Then it gives place to other modes.

That is the quite invariable process with all the products and all the methods, of all the arts. But naturally, as the arts grow older, their practitioners have a better chance of evolving newer and sounder methods, for the number of their predecessors has inevitably increased. Bunyan must evolve his method for himself; Defoe could study Bunyan; Richardson, Bunyan and Defoe; Diderot, Richardson and his predecessors; Stendhal could draw on the experience of four generations; Flaubert on that of five; Conrad on that of six. This of course is a source of danger to weaker brethren, for in each generation an enormous amount of insipid art is turned out by inferior students receiving their instruction at the hands of academic instructors. That cannot be helped. But the fact remains that to a real master possessed of a real individuality the study of the methods of his predecessors must be of enormous use. Anyone at all instructed, reading the work of

Conrad, must find evidence of an almost life-long and almost incredibly minute study of writers preceding him and the amount of reading and of study—for they are not the same thing—that must have gone to the making of the author of *Ulysses*, who is certainly the greatest of all prose virtuosi of the word—that beggars the imagination!

So it happened that in France from, say, the 'fifties to the early 'nineties of the last century, you had a place of dignity found for the hitherto despised Novel—and in consequence you very speedily found an accepted convention. For once an occupation is discovered to be dignified you will very soon find that investigators of methods are at work upon it. The game of marbles was, in my hey-day, regarded as an occupation solely for little boys; but with the institution some few years ago of an international championship it came in for the most serious of study by grown men, and the photographs of last year's world-contest that a little time ago filled the public prints, showed the competitors to be white-headed, grey-bearded, or very rotund of figure. The champion was eventually found, as far as I can remember, in a gentleman of sixty and over.

So with *Le Rouge et le Noir* it became evident to the world that the novel of discussion or of investigation was a possibility and, with that discovery, the great novels began to come. The discussions to be found in the very few works of fiction by Diderot were naturally experimental and amateurish. Like Richardson he was tremendously on the side of the more or less patriarchal and civic angels. Nevertheless, he could give you a parasite talking in favour of his profession or a rogue justifying his courses with a sincerity and a reasonable ingenuousness that differed extremely from the exaggerated speeches of the villains of the Fielding, the Dickens, or the commercial, nuvvle. Stendhal, on the other hand, being what one might call a cold Nietzschean—or it might be more just to say that Nietzsche was a warmed-up Stendhalean—Stendhal, then, swung the balance rather to the other extreme, tending to make his detrimentals argumentatively masterly and his conventionally virtuous characters banal and impotent.

At any rate, with or after Stendhal, it became evident that, if the novel was to have what is called *vraisemblance*, if it was so to render life as to engross its reader, the novelist must not take sides either with the virtuous whose virtues cause them to prosper or with the vicious whose very virtues drive them always nearer and nearer to the gallows or the pauper's grave. That does not say that the author need abstain from letting his conventionally virtuous characters prosper to any thinkable extent. For however scientifically the matter be considered, material if not intellectual honesty, sobriety, continence, frugality, parsimony, and the other material virtues will give any man a better chance of fourteen thousand—pounds or dollars—a year than if he should be, however intellectually honest, financially unsound, or a drunkard or a dreamer or one who never talks about the baths he takes. The publisher, in fact, has a better chance of both terrestrial and skyey mansions than the novelist.

Nevertheless, the novelist must not, by taking sides, exhibit his preferences. He must not show his publisher as all shining benevolence and well-soaped chastity without pointing out that his fellows, the unwashed, incontinent, wastrel Villons of the world, sometimes practise Robin Hoodish generosities and sometimes smooth with their works the pillows of the agonized and sleepless.

And in between the starving Chatterton and the august house of, say, Longmans, Norton, Hurst, Rees, and Co.—who did not publish Chatterton—he must place and set in motion the teeming world of averagely sensual, averagely kindly, averagely cruel, averagely honest, averagely imbecile human beings whose providentially appointed mission would seem to be to turn into the stuff that fills graveyards. So that it is not so much the function of the novelist to hold the balance straight as, dispensing with all scales or instruments for measuring, to show all the human beings of his creation going about their avocations. He has, that is to say, to render and not to tell. (If I say, " The wicked Mr. Blank shot nice Blanche's dear cat ! " that is telling. If I say : " Blank raised his rifle and aimed it at the quivering, black-burdened topmost bough of the cherry-tree. After the report a spattered bunch of scarlet and black quiverings dropped from branch to branch to pancake itself on the orchard grass ! " that is rather bad rendering, but still rendering. Or if I say Monsieur Chose was a vulgar, coarse, obese and presumptuous fellow—that is telling. But if I say, " He was a gentleman with red whiskers that always preceded him through a doorway," there you have him rendered—as Maupassant rendered him.)

It was Flaubert who most shiningly preached the doctrine of the novelist as Creator who should have a Creator's aloofness, rendering the world as he sees it, uttering no comments, falsifying no issues and carrying the subject —the Affair—he has selected for rendering, remorselessly out to its logical conclusion.

There came thus into existence the novel of Aloofness. It had even in France something of a struggle for that existence and the author of *Madame Bovary* which was the first great novel logically—and indeed passionately—to carry out this theory, had to face a criminal prosecution because in the opinion of the Government of Napoleon III a book that is not actively on the side of constituted authority and of established morality is of necessity dangerous to morals and subversive of good government.

That view—it is still largely entertained by the academic critics of Anglo-Saxondom—is of course imbecile, but it is not without a certain basis in the sentiments of common humanity. It is normal for poor, badgered men to desire to read of a sort of representative type who, as hero of a book, shall triumph over all obstacles with surprising ease and as if with the backing of a deity. In that way they can dream of easy ends for themselves. So they will dislike authors who do not side with their own types. And as constituted governments and academic bodies are made up of what the French call *hommes moyen sensuels*, such corporations will do what they can to prevent novelists from not taking sides with agreeable characters.

To the theory of Aloofness added itself, by a very natural process, the other theory that the story of a novel should be the history of an Affair and not a tale in which a central character with an attendant female should be followed through a certain space of time until the book comes to a happy end on a note of matrimony or to an unhappy end—represented by a death. That latter —the normal practice of the earlier novelist and still the normal expedient of the novel of commerce or of escape—is again imbecile, but again designed to satisfy a very natural human desire for finality. We have a natural desire to be kidded into thinking that for nice agreeable persons like ourselves life will finally bring us to a stage where an admirably planned villa, a sempiternally charming—and yet changing—companion, and a sufficiency of bathrooms, automobiles, gramophones, radios, and grand pianos to establish us well in the forefront of the class to which we hope to belong, shall witness the long, uneventful, fortunate and effortless closing years of our lives. And our desire to be kidded into that belief is all the stronger in that whenever we do examine with any minuteness into the lives of our fellow human beings practically nothing of the sort ever happens to them. So we say : "Life is too sad for us to want to read books that remind us of it ! "

But that is the justification for the novel of Aloofness, rendering not the arbitrary felicities of a central character but the singular normalities of an Affair. Normal humanity, deprived of the possibility of viewing either lives or life, makes naturally for a pessimism that demands relief either in the drugs of the happy endings of falsified fictions or in the anodynes of superstition—one habit being as fatal to the human intelligence as the other. But there is no need to entertain the belief that life is sad any more than there is any benefit to be derived from the contemplation of fictitious and banal joys. The French peasant long ago evolved the rule that life is never either as good or as bad as one expects it to be and so the French peasant, like every proper man, faces life with composure—and reads *Madame Bovary*, whilst the English, say, lawyer has never got beyond *The Three Musketeers*.

The progress from the one to the other is simple and logical enough. If you no longer allow yourself to take sides with your characters you begin very soon to see that such a thing as a hero does not exist—a discovery that even Thackeray could make. And, from there to seeing that it is not individuals but enterprises or groups that succeed or fail is a very small step to take. And then immediately there suggests itself the other fact that it is not the mere death and still less the mere marriage of an individual that brings to an end either a group or an enterprise. It is perhaps going too far to say that *no* man is indispensable, but it is far more usual to find that, when a seemingly indispensable individual disappears for one reason or another from an enterprise, that adventure proceeds with equanimity and very little shock. I suppose the most co-operative and at the same time the most one-man concern of to-

day is the newspaper or the periodical publication, and I suppose that in my time I must
have been acquainted with something at least
of the affairs of at least a hundred journals or
periodicals each of them of necessity more or
less autocratically conducted, simply because
a journal running along and having to appear
on a stated day, it is hardly ever practicable
to get together an editorial committee soon
enough to make momentous decisions that
may have to be arrived at in a minute or two.
Yet almost the first discovery that the most
strong-minded of editors makes after he has
got the periodical of his founding running
for a month or two is that it is the periodical
that has taken charge—and the most notable
fact of journalism is that even when the most
noted of editors suddenly dies his paper in
the immense majority of cases goes on running
in perfect tranquillity and with no apparent
change for a period sufficiently long to make
it perfectly manifest that the great man was
not in the least indispensable.

And, as with newspapers, so with nearly
all the other enterprises of life. I am not of
course saying that no great man exists or no
founder of great enterprises, though I should
imagine that there must be even more mute

inglorious Miltons than ever got a chance of putting their epics before the public. Still, the evolver of a new process or a revived combination does exist and not infrequently does get his chance : and there is no particular reason why the serious novelist should not select the Affair of a successful individual for treatment. That he seldom does so is usually because, having studied the cases of successful men, he is apt to come to the conclusion that they are not unseldom neither edifying as histories nor psychologically very interesting. Alexander, that is to say, may have sighed for new worlds to conquer, but it is probable that he would have bartered several of his empires for the certainty of a little peace at his own fireside and an improved digestion.

Flaubert, then, gave us *Madame Bovary*, which may be described as the first great novel that aimed at aloofness. That it did not succeed in its aim, Flaubert being in the end so fascinated by his Emma that beside her and the ingenuous weakness of her genuine romanticism every other character in the book is either hypocritical, mean or meanly imbecile—that it did not succeed in that aim is not to be wondered at when we consider the great, buoyant, and essentially optimist figure that he was. And indeed, all authors being men, it is very unlikely that the completely aloof novel will ever see the light. If you want to be a novelist you must first be a poet and it is impossible to be a poet and lack human sympathies or generosity of outlook. In *Education Senti-mentale*—which, if I had to decide the matter, though fortunately I don't, I should call the greatest novel ever written—the author of *Madame Bovary* gave us a nearly perfect group novel, written from a standpoint of very nearly complete aloofness. In *Bouvard et Pécuchet*, abandoning as it were human measures of success and failure, he takes as his hero the imbecility of co-operative mankind and as his heroine the futility of the accepted idea, and, being thus as it were detached from the earth and its standards, he could draw in Bouvard and his mate, two of the most lovable of human beings that ever set out upon a forlorn hope. He died in the attempt.

The Flaubert school or group lasted sufficiently long in France, though, after the late War, its influence was completely washed out by a sort of eclecticism whose main features it is very difficult to trace and into whose ramifications I do not intend to enter, for it has had practically no time to influence the work of Anglo-Saxon novel writers. Flaubert, Maupassant, Turgenev, the Gourmonts, Daudet, and the rest of those who had their places at Brébant's died in their allotted years, the last survivor of any prominence being Anatole France, whose death was greeted by an outburst of furious hatred in France such as can seldom have greeted the passing of a distinguished figure. That was because the French young, saddened and rendered starving by the War which just preceded France's death, turned with loathing from the rather *débonnaire* aloofness of the author of *Histoire Comique*. And indeed if we Anglo-Saxons had suffered in the least as much as those Latins I might well expect to find myself lynched for writing what I have done above. I have seldom witnessed anything to equal the dismay of a great French gathering of *littérateurs* when their honoured guest, an English novelist of distinction and indeed of internationally public literary functions, told them in quite immaculate French that all he knew of writing he had from France, and that all that he had from France he had learned from the works of Guy de Maupassant! If he had gone round that great assembly and had, with his glove, flicked each one of the guests in the face, he could not have caused greater consternation. Nevertheless it is true that Maupassant must have had more influence on the Anglo-Saxon writer of to-day than any other writer of fiction, Henry James possibly excepted.

In England, meantime, slightly before the 1890's, the solid vogue of—or the somnolent rumination over—the three-volumed nuvvle of commerce had been seriously threatened by the slow spread of the idea that writing might be an art, by a tremendous drop in the prices at which books might be sold and by revolutionary attacks on Victorian conventional morality. The loosening in morality need not concern us except in so far as it shook the idea that the novelist must of necessity colour all his characters with one or other hue, but the drop in the price of books facilitated at least all sorts of experimental adventures. Whilst the nuvvle remained a thirty-shilling three-decker publishers must needs play for safety whether in morals or methods and neither, say, the *Hill-top* novels of Grant Allen, which were pseudo-scientific attacks on conventional morality, nor yet *Almayer's Folly*, which was an attempt to

[131]

introduce the artistic standards and methods of Flaubert into Anglo-Saxondom, could have had even the remotest chance of publication had the novel remained at its former price.

On the other hand, such writers as Wilde, Stevenson, Pater, and Meredith did, dealing mostly in verbal felicities or infelicities, begin rather vaguely to perceive that writing was an art. Neither Wilde nor Pater were novelists in the sense of devoting the greater part of their time or energies to the art of fiction, and Stevenson remained an avowed moralist, whilst Meredith devoted himself to large national aspirations—which have nothing to do with art. And all the four, as I have said, were essentially rather stylists *tels quels* than anything else. When Pater, Wilde, or Meredith had succeeded in a passage in showing what clever fellows they were they were satisfied and Stevenson, if he had some conception of how to tell a story, was far more gratified if he had succeeded in producing a quaint sentence with turns of phrase after the manner of Sir Thomas Browne than intent on the fact that every sentence —nay, every word!—should carry on the effect of the story to be told.

But the mere fact that writers were then

beginning to pay some attention to manner rather than to matter or morals—that they were intent on being writers rather than gentlemen—that mere fact is one to excite lively gratitude in lands like ours and the job of being a novelist is one of such excruciating difficulty that it would be ungrateful to ask of pioneers that they should be more than pioneers.

The effect of their propaganda almost more than of their achievements, combined with the cheapening of books and the impingement on Anglo-Saxon shores of French examples of how things should be done—for it was not until the late 'eighties that Flaubert, Maupassant, and Turgenev really produced any overwhelming effect in either England or the United States—the effect then of all these factors coming almost together was an outburst of technical effort such as can have rarely been witnessed in any other race or time. The idea that writing was an art and as such had its dignity, that it had methods to be studied and was therefore such another acknowledged craft as is shoe-making—such ideas acted for a time, in the days of the *Yellow Book*, like magic on a whole horde of English—and still more of American—writers.

I have of course not here the space to go with any minuteness into the history of the *Yellow Book* period. Founded by two Americans—Henry James and Henry Harland—in London where circumstances were certainly more favourable than they would have been in, say, New York or Boston, the *Yellow Book* did undoubtedly promote an interest in technical matters that hardly any other periodical or Movement could have done. James was a direct pupil of Turgenev; Harland and most of the contributors to the periodical were products rather of a general " Frenchness " than the students of any one author—the products of a blend of Mallarmé, Mérimée, Murger, and Maupassant and a Quartier Latin frame of mind and personal untidiness.

Its defect as a movement was that its supporters, also, probably aimed rather at displaying personal cleverness than at the concealment of themselves beneath the surfaces of their works. They had not yet learnt the sternest of all lessons—that the story is the thing, and the story and then the story, and that there is nothing else that matters in the world.

IN THE LAST QUARTER OF
A CENTURY

WHEN the dust of the *Yellow Book* period
died away with the trial and disappearance of Wilde there did nevertheless
remain in the public and the literary mind
some conception that novel-writing was an
art and that the novel was a vehicle by means
of which every kind of psychological or scien-
tific truth connected with human life and
affairs could be very fittingly conveyed. To-
day I imagine that there would not be many
found to deny that it is the vehicle by means
of which those truths can be most fittingly
investigated. To that we may some day
return.

In the meantime the *Yellow Book* period
also left behind it three men whose names
must for ever stand out for the student of the
history of the English Novel—they were
Henry James, Stephen Crane, and Joseph

Conrad. I do not purpose here to attempt an estimate of any one of the three; I merely wish to point out what it was that distinguished them from all of their predecessors and nearly all of their distinguished contemporaries. Their distinguished contemporaries are all, most fortunately, still alive and so beyond the reach of my pen—but it must, I imagine, he fairly obvious that, say, Mr. Wells, Mr. Kipling, Mr. Galsworthy, or Mr. Arnold Bennett are each solitary figures, ploughing lonely furrows and expressing their admirable selves in admirable ways known only to themselves.

About that other triad there was a certain solidarity, a certain oneness of method and even a certain comradeship. They lived in the same corner of England, saw each other often and discussed literary methods more thoroughly and more frequently than can ever at any other time in England have been the case. To be sure, not one of the three was English.

Indeed, some ten years or so ago my friend Mr. Wells wrote to the papers to say that in the first decade of this century a group of foreigners occupied that corner of England and were engaged in plotting against the English novel. At the time that appeared. to be the sort of patriotic nonsense that occupied our minds a good deal just after the War—but Mr. Wells, as usual, was right. The extent of the conspiracy was this : the works of those three writers whose influence on the Anglo-Saxon—and even to some extent on the British—novel was overwhelming—were united by a common technique and their literary aims were to all intents exactly the same.

All three treated their characters with aloofness ; all three kept themselves, their comments and their prejudices out of their works, and all three rendered rather than told. On the whole those characteristics which never before characterized the English novel characterize it to-day. No one, that is, would to-day set out to capture the suffrages of either the more instructed or of even the almost altogether naïf with a novel of the type of those written by the followers of Bunyan, Defoe, Fielding, Charles Reade, or William Black. No author would, like Thackeray, to-day intrude his broken nose and myopic spectacles into the middle of the most thrilling scene he ever wrote, in order to tell you that, though his heroine was rather a wrong 'un, his own heart was in his right place.

James, Conrad, and Crane differed from each other in minute points and indeed in broader characteristics. James was more introspective, Crane more incisive in his writing, Conrad more nearly approached the ordinary definition of the poet and was less remorselessly aloof than either of the others. But their common, Gallic origin united them, so that they had before all for their strongest passion the desire to convey vicarious experience to the reader. Conrad wrote of his literary aim: "It is above all to make you see," and Crane might have written the same thing had he ever written about himself. And Henry James might have written if he could ever have brought himself to write anything so unqualified about his aims: "It is above all to make you feel!" At any rate, the common aim was to take the reader, immerse him in an Affair so completely that he was unconscious either of the fact that he was reading or of the identity of the author, so that in the end he might say— and believe: "I have been in a drawing-room overlooking Boston Common, in a drinking saloon in Yellow Sky or beneath the palm leaves of Palembang! I *have* been!"

At this aim, to which they certainly attained, they arrived by certain technical devices or rules. Most of these I have already fore-shadowed and as I am not here writing a technical work, I do not propose to go into the others at all closely. The only sound technical rules are those that are founded on a study of what pleases : if what you write is to please you must see how your predecessors did it. There can be nothing either highbrow or recondite about your efforts ; the nearer you are to your fellow-man who differs from you only in not having literary ambitions or gifts, the nearer you are to universality ; the nearer you are to univer-sality the greater you are, the more nearly you will have justified your existence.

You must therefore write as simply as you can—with the extreme of the simplicity that is granted to you, and you must write of subjects that spring at your throat. But why subjects appeal to you you have no means of knowing. The appeal of the subject is nevertheless the only thing that is open to your native genius—the only thing as to which you can say : " I cannot help it : that is what appealed to me!" You must never, after that, say: "I write like this because I want to," but you must say: "I write like this because I hope it is what the unspoiled reader likes!"

Having got your subject you will, if you are prudent, live with it for a long, long time before you sit down to write it. During that time you will be doing at odd moments what Conrad used to call "squeezing the guts out of it." For it is a mistake to think that what looks like the rendering of an ordinary affair is ever an artless chronicling. Your "subject" may be just the merest nothing in the way of intrigue or plot—but to the merest nothings in human affairs all the intrigues of the universe have contributed since first this earth swung away, a drop of molten metal, from the first of all principles. Your "subject" might be no more than a child catching frogs in a swamp or the emotions of a nervous woman in a thunderstorm, but all the history of the world has gone to putting child or woman where they are and up to either subject you might lead with an epic as thrilling in its end as that of *Othello* or an episode as poignant with absolute relief as came to the world on the eleventh of

November, 1918. You have at your dis-
posal heredity, environment, the concatena-
tion of the effects of the one damn thing
after another that life is—and Destiny who
is blind and august. Those are the colours of
your palette : it is for you to see that line
by line and filament of colour by filament,
the reader's eye is conducted to your cul-
minating point.

That is, then, all that I have to say of the
gradual progress of the English novel—to
the point where it becomes the Novel. I
have traced out as plainly as I could the lines
of the pattern as it appears to me and the
reader must use that pattern for what jumpings
off of his own he chooses to make.

That this is not the final stage of the Novel
is obvious ; there will be developments that
we cannot foresee, strain our visions how we
may. There are probably—humanity being
stable, change the world how it may—there
are probably eternal principles for all the arts,
but the applications of those principles are
eternally changing, or eternally revolving. It
is, for instance, an obvious and unchanging
fact that if an author intrudes his comments
into the middle of his story he will endanger
the illusion conveyed by that story—but a

generation of readers may come along who would prefer witnessing the capers of the author to being carried away by stories and that generation of readers may coincide with a generation of writers tired of self-obliteration. So you might have a world of Oscar Wildes or of Lylys. Or you might, again, have a world tired of the really well constructed novel every word of which carries its story forward : then you will have a movement towards diffuseness, backboneless sentences, digressions, and inchoatenesses.

But, for the moment, the outline that I have traced for you seems to have got about as far as we ourselves have.

AN AFTERWORD
C. H. SISSON

FORD is an irresponsible writer, in the sense that you cannot rely on the accuracy of his statements. What does 'absolute truth as to the impression'—a favourite phrase of his—mean except that what he records is how things seem to him, without regard to anything so awkward as objective fact? Yet his reputation as a liar has been much exaggerated. His impressions are undoubtedly more worth taking account of than most people's, and where he claims to have seen something there does indeed prove to be something to be seen. There may be other aspects of the matter in hand, not taken account of by him, but the aspect that has struck him is perfectly real and often important. In a writer of fiction, even of memoirs, this may be accepted as enough, but what of criticism? We are certainly used to critics who claim a comprehensive view of things, and there are certainly kinds of criticism which require more attention to what are ordinarily thought of as facts than Ford ever bothered his head about.

A book with the title, *The English Novel, from the Earliest Days to the Death of Joseph Conrad*, might seem to be in that class—and it would be, if Ford were trying to give us anything like a

[143]

comprehensive history. That is, however, not
what is here on offer. So, unless the reader is one
of those who think that to get a fact wrong is
always criminal—as it certainly is always a mild
nuisance at least—he should pass lightly over the
few patent inaccuracies in this book, such as the
confusion between Henry and Thomas Vaughan,
and about their dates, or the substitution in one
place of Gourmont for Goncourt, which may be
a printer's error. Ford tells us that he wrote the
book at various times and places between 1927
and 1930, partly 'on board the *S.S.Patria* and
in the port and neighbourhood of Marseilles'.
It is as if to warn us that he was writing out of
his head, as he certainly was, and without con-
sulting libraries. That particular head did, however, contain an immense amount of knowledge
about the novel. Ford had written a score of
novels of his own, including several which are
among the best of the century; he had discussed
the problems and techniques of the novel at
length with Conrad and others and he had, from
childhood onwards, read an immense number of
novels, from the acknowledged classics to the
miscellaneous apprentice work on which he was
always being called to advise.

What he has given us in *The English Novel* is
not a history but a genial and high-spirited outpouring from a mind not only full of his subject
but loving it. Ford is an enthusiast who tells us

recklessly what he likes and what he doesn't. Though his dislikes—for the moral attitudes of Fielding or for the social attitudes which once tempted writers to prefer to be thought of as gentlemen—are energetic, they are occasional. The book is dominated by his likes, and the tips he gives are, as is usual with him, good ones. Captain Marryat, for example, is presumably now in the depths of unfashionableness, but *Peter Simple* is certainly one of the best novels in the language. But what Ford conveys above all is less his particular preference than his radical passion for the novel as an instrument and for what can be done with it. He is far from trying to thrust this or that author down anyone's throat. The width of his sympathies is remarkable, and he wants the reader to pick and choose for himself as he has picked and chosen, but also to know how wide the choice really is. He is frank about the boringness of what has bored him. He does not want to be taken too literally, but his most throwaway statements are serious pointers to matters which merit consideration; as when he says that 'from the death of Swift to the publication of *The Way of All Flesh* there is very little to be found in the English novel that is not slightly unworthy of the attention of a grown-up man—say of a grown-up Frenchman'. It is the cosiness and sentimentality, and the social pretences, which dominate so much of

[145]

our best-known fiction that he is pointing to.
Dickens with all his genius was a fuddy-duddy
in comparison with Swift or—to go outside the
field of fiction—Sir Walter Raleigh. Ford thought
that this superior degree of adulthood and knowledge of the human heart should find its way into
the novel. He believed that these possibilities
were not unconnected with that escape from the
shapelessness of so much English fiction which
he saw as having been achieved with James and
Conrad, under the tutelage of Stendhal and above
all Flaubert. At the same time he appreciated the
cross-currents which had resulted in the English
novel—through the medium of Richardson—
having influenced in turn Diderot and Stendhal
himself.

It is true that the moralisms which disfigured
so many novels in the nineteenth century have
disappeared like morning dew, but before we
congratulate ourselves too loudly on that account
we should consider how far their place has been
taken by obsessing imperatives which may be
equally blinding. However the prescriptions of
the libertarian moralities now fashionable may
differ from those of a more shamelessly bourgeois
world, they can have much the same effect in
impeding observation. Passionate believers in the
rights of people to do this or that, passionate
advocates of this or that social attitude, suffer
like their predecessors from thinking that they

[146]

know what is there before they look. For Ford the essence of the novel was a recording of how individual people actually behave. He saw this as a civilising function, a source of knowledge which told against all sorts of political tendentiousness. Of course the novelist, like anybody else, might as a social person have strong views about any of the issues of the day, but that must not stop him seeing what was in front of his nose because he feared consequences for whatever cause he had espoused. In Ford's view of things the shaping of a novel meant the working out of an 'affair'—any situation in which people move from one state of inter-relationship to another, not necessarily a more conclusive one. That, as he saw it, is how life is.

Ford would not have expected the perspectives of a reader of the 1980s to be the same as those of himself and his contemporaries in 1930. 'One must,' he says, 'live in, one must face the circumstances of one's own age.' He had faced the consequences of an increase in the speed of transport and the unsettling of local communities, but he did not know our world in which most people get their entertainment mainly from television, and are in the habit of being entertained by fabricated materials to an extent and for durations unprecedented in the history of the human race. It may be said that, as a primary form of entertainment, the novel has been entirely superseded, having held that position for barely a couple of centuries. That does not mean that it need not continue to entertain; indeed all art must do that, whatever else it does or does not do. It may mean that the temptations of aiming at a sentimental and tendentious public, so marked in the nineteenth century, will no longer be there. Meanwhile novels of the older type—say, Trollope's—not only provide matter for the mostly rather second-hand world of television, where the money now is, but find in that popular audience some readers who would not otherwise find their way to the books. 'As seen on television' can be an advertisement for more than soap-powders. And for those who do actually read novels, Ford's uninhibited expression of likes and dislikes will point usefully to where the riches lie, 'from the earliest days to the death of Joseph Conrad', and to the essential qualities of the novel which are instinctively sought out by those readers for whom truth of some kind is an essential ingredient of entertainment of any kind.

FORD MADOX FORD

FORD MADOX FORD (the name he adopted in 1919: he was originally Ford Hermann Hueffer) was born in 1873 in Merton, Surrey. His father, Francis Hueffer, who was an author and musicologist, died when Ford was fifteen. Ford's mother, Catherine, was the daughter of the Pre-Raphaelite painter Ford Madox Brown. Ford quickly took to writing: his first book, a children's fairy-tale, was published when he was seventeen, and his first novel, *The Shifting of the Fire*, came out in 1892. After the death of Ford Madox Brown in 1893, Ford wrote a biography of his grandfather, which was published in 1896. He was therefore an experienced author before (now married to Elsie Martindale) he encountered Joseph Conrad in 1898, and began a literary relationship which proved highly fruitful for the development of both writers' conception of the novelist's task. Conrad and Ford collaborated on *The Inheritors* (1901) and other books, and Ford wrote an instalment of *Nostromo* when Conrad was too ill to meet the deadline. Ford continued to write prolifically on his own account in a variety of forms: art criticism (books on Rossetti and Hans Holbein in 1902 and 1905), poetry, essays and novels. His trilogy of historical novels about Henry VIII and Katherine Howard began with *The Fifth Queen* in 1906, followed by *Privy Seal* in 1907 and *The Fifth Queen Crowned* in 1908. In 1908, he founded the *English Review*, which proved a literary success if a financial failure, publishing work by many major writers (such as Conrad, Hardy, Wells, James, Bennett and Forster) and helping to begin the careers of such as Wyndham Lewis and Lawrence. Ford's complicated private life became a matter of public notoriety when first *The Daily Mirror* and then a magazine called *The Throne* referred to Violet Hunt, for whom Ford had left his wife, as Mrs Hueffer, and Elsie set in train legal proceedings. Meanwhile, Ford's literary output continued with further novels (including *A Call* in 1910), his *Collected Poems* in 1913, and a critical study of

Henry James. He wrote the novel which he called his best book, *The Good Soldier*, in 1913–14, and it was published in 1915. In the same year, Ford took a commission in the army. His experience of the battle of the Somme in 1916, during which he was wounded, furnished him with material for his Tietjens tetralogy, *Parade's End*, which began with the publication of *Some Do Not* in 1924. By then Ford had begun a relationship with Stella Bowen, by whom he had a daughter (he had two previous daughters by Elsie Martindale), had moved to France, and had begun to edit the *Transatlantic Review*. This journal published the work of, among others, Pound, Gertrude Stein, Hemingway and Joyce. A book of reminiscences of Joseph Conrad was published in 1924; the second Tietjens novel, *No More Parades*, in 1925; the third, *A Man Could Stand Up*, in 1926; and the fourth, *The Last Post*, in 1928. His critical study, *The English Novel*, appeared in 1929. Having separated from Stella Bowen and had an affair with Jean Rhys, whose work he published in the *Transatlantic Review*, Ford met Janice Biala in 1930, and lived with her until his death in 1939. He continued to publish novels regularly, as well as other works, notably an extended *Collected Poems* in 1936.

ALSO BY FORD MADOX FORD FROM CARCANET

The Rash Act
A History of Our Own Times
Ladies Whose Bright Eyes
The Ford Reader